THE AGE OF REVOLUTION

THE FRENCH REVOLUTION, NAPOLEON, AND THE REPUBLIC

LIBERTÉ, ÉGALITÉ, FRATERNITÉ

EDITED BY
JEREMY KLAR

Britannica
Educational Publishing
IN ASSOCIATION WITH
ROSEN
EDUCATIONAL SERVICES

Published in 2016 by Britannica Educational Publishing (a trademark of Encyclopædia Britannica, Inc.) in association with The Rosen Publishing Group, Inc.
29 East 21st Street, New York, NY 10010

Copyright © 2016 by Encyclopædia Britannica, Inc. Britannica, Encyclopædia Britannica, and the Thistle logo are registered trademarks of Encyclopædia Britannica, Inc. All rights reserved.

Rosen Publishing materials copyright © 2016 The Rosen Publishing Group, Inc. All rights reserved.

Distributed exclusively by Rosen Publishing.
To see additional Britannica Educational Publishing titles, go to rosenpublishing.com.

First Edition

Britannica Educational Publishing
J. E. Luebering: Director, Core Reference Group
Anthony L. Green: Editor, Compton's by Britannica

Rosen Publishing
Hope Lourie Killcoyne: Executive Editor
Jeremy Klar: Editor
Nelson Sá: Art Director
Michael Moy: Designer
Cindy Reiman: Photography Manager
Introduction and conclusion by Emily Swanson.

Library of Congress Cataloging-in-Publication Data

The French Revolution, Napoleon, and the Republic: liberté, égalité, fraternité/edited by Jeremy Klar.—First edition.
    pages cm.—(The age of revolution)
Includes bibliographical references and index.
ISBN 978-1-68048-023-8 (library bound)
1. France—History—Revolution, 1789-1799—Juvenile literature. I. Klar, Jeremy.
DC148.F726 2016
944.04—dc23

2014038138

Manufactured in the United States of America

Photo credits: Cover, p. 1 DEA Picture Library/Getty Images; pp. xii, 50–51 Heritage Images/Hulton Fine Art Collection/Getty Images; pp. 4, 66, 67, 127 Encyclopædia Britannica, Inc.; p. 7 Leemage/Hulton Fine Art Collection/Getty Images; p. 13 Musee de la Marine, Paris, France/De Agostini Picture Library/M. Seemuller/Bridgeman Images; p. 14 DEA/M. Seemuller/De Agostini/Getty Images; pp. 17, 46 AISA - Everett/Shutterstock.com; pp. 20, 55, 91, 111 © Photos.com/Thinkstock; pp. 26–27, 125 Library of Congress, Washington, D.C.; pp. 30–31, 75 Private Collection/© Look and Learn/Bridgeman Images; p. 32, 95 Classic Vision/age fotostock/SuperStock; p. 37 Leeimage/Universal Images Group/Getty Images; p. 39 National Gallery of Art, Washington, Timken Collection; p. 64, 86 Private Collection/Bridgeman Images; p. 81 Universal Images Group/Getty Images; p. 105 DeAgostini/SuperStock; pp. 112–113 Jastrow; p. 117 DEA/A. Dagli Orti/De Agostini/Getty Images p. 133 Print Collector/Hulton Archive/Getty Images.

CONTENTS

INTRODUCTION.. vi

CHAPTER 1

PREREVOLUTIONARY FRANCE 1

SOCIAL AND POLITICAL HERITAGE..................... 2
THE SOCIAL ORDER OF THE ANCIEN RÉGIME..................... 2
MONARCHY AND CHURCH 5
COMMITMENT TO MODERNIZATION......................... 6
LETTRES DE CACHET 8

CONTINUITY AND CHANGE.......................... 10
AGRICULTURAL PATTERNS......................... 11
INDUSTRIAL PRODUCTION 12
COMMERCE 14
CITIES 16

CULTURAL TRANSFORMATION 16
THE INFLUENCE OF MONTESQUIEU AND ROUSSEAU............. 18

CHAPTER 2

CAUSES OF THE REVOLUTION............... 24
FOREIGN POLICY AND FINANCIAL CRISIS.............. 25
DOMESTIC POLICY AND REFORM EFFORTS 28
TAX REFORM.. 31
PARLEMENTS 33

  THE TAILLE AND CAPITATION TAXES 34
 KING AND *PARLEMENTS* 36
  AFFAIR OF THE DIAMOND NECKLACE 40
 THE BUILDUP TO REVOLUTION 43

CHAPTER 3
THE DESTRUCTION OF THE ANCIEN RÉGIME 48
 THE CONVERGENCE OF REVOLUTIONS, 1789 49
  THE JURIDICAL REVOLUTION 49
  PARISIAN REVOLT 53
   THE FLAG OF FRANCE 56
  PEASANT INSURGENCIES 57
  THE ABOLITION OF FEUDALISM 59
 THE NEW REGIME 60
  RESTRUCTURING FRANCE 61
  SALE OF NATIONAL LANDS 68
 SEEDS OF DISCORD 70
  RELIGIOUS TENSIONS 71
  POLITICAL TENSIONS 72

CHAPTER 4
THE FIRST FRENCH REPUBLIC 79
 THE SECOND REVOLUTION 79
 A REPUBLIC IN CRISIS 82
 GIRONDINS AND MONTAGNARDS 83
 THE REIGN OF TERROR 88
 THE JACOBIN DICTATORSHIP 92

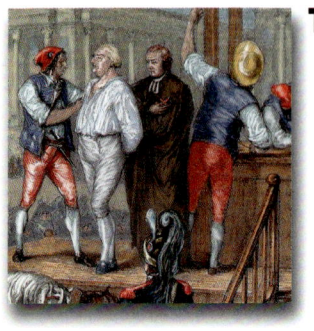

FRENCH REPUBLICAN CALENDAR *92*
THE ARMY OF THE REPUBLIC. 96
THE THERMIDORIAN REACTION. 98
THE DIRECTORY. 100
    FRANÇOIS-NOËL BABEUF 101
        SISTER REPUBLICS 103
        ALIENATION AND COUPS. 106

CHAPTER 5
THE NAPOLEONIC ERA 109
    THE CONSULATE 110
    LOSS OF POLITICAL FREEDOM. 114
    SOCIETY IN NAPOLEONIC FRANCE. 115
        RELIGIOUS POLICY. 116
        NAPOLEONIC NOBILITY 119
        THE CIVIL CODE 120
            THE NAPOLEONIC CODE BEYOND FRANCE 122
    CAMPAIGNS AND CONQUESTS, 1797–1807. 123
    THE GRAND EMPIRE 126
    THE CONTINENTAL SYSTEM. 126
    CONSCRIPTION 129
    NAPOLEON AND THE REVOLUTION. 131

CONCLUSION. 135
GLOSSARY. 137
BIBLIOGRAPHY. 140
INDEX 144

INTRODUCTION

On the morning of July 14, 1789, a Parisian crowd advanced on the Bastille—a medieval fortress on the east side of Paris—demanding the release of the arms and munitions stored there. In the 17th and 18th centuries, the Bastille had become not only a state prison and a place of detention for important persons charged with various offenses. Beyond its role as a prison, the Bastille had also become a symbol of the despotism of the ruling Bourbon monarchy. Angered by the prison governor's evasiveness, the people stormed and captured the place—an action that came to symbolize the end of the French monarchic regime and its social institutions.

The French Revolution is considered by most historians to mark the definitive end of the premodern era in France. Although the revolutionary fervour began in 1787, it reached its definitive climax in 1789 with the fall of the Bastille, and did not end until the late 1790s with the rise of Napoleon Bonaparte. Inspired by the Enlightenment ideas of such philosophers as Jean-Jacques Rousseau and René Descartes, the French revolutionaries overthrew the oppressive systems of feudalism and absolute monarchy in favour of secularized individualism, representative government, and constitutionally defined inalienable rights.

While it is largely remembered for its devolutions at times into infighting and what essentially amounted to bloodbaths, the French Revolution's true impact

INTRODUCTION

was its influence in giving form to our modern understanding of democracy and citizenship. The French Revolution sent a message not just through France but in fact to the whole world that the essential sovereignty of the individual and the political might of the masses could not be ignored.

With the fall of the Bastille in 1789, the French Revolution was undeniably underway, however, the revolution was not born overnight; it was in fact the culmination of decades of political unrest and economic instability. The French economy had been devastated by the excessive spending of Louis XVI and the country's involvement in the American Revolution. While providing aid to American revolutionaries enhanced French prestige, the country won no land or economic gains through their involvement, and as a result, France was burdened with loans it couldn't repay and, a seriously battered economy.

The peasant class had also endured years of severe famine and economic hardships brought on by droughts and a particularly violent hailstorm that devastated the country's crops. An unusually cold winter in 1788 caused rivers to freeze, slowing the trade and transport of flour and other staples. As a result, the price of bread—the main form of sustenance for most of the population—nearly doubled. The immediate threat of food shortages and the economic disenfranchisement of the peasants, combined with changing understandings of citizenry and a public inspired by Enlightenment philosophy, set the stage for revolution.

By the fall of 1786 peasant riots had begun to spring up throughout the countryside. In an attempt to appease the

THE FRENCH REVOLUTION, NAPOLEON, AND THE REPUBLIC:
LIBERTÉ, ÉGALITÉ, AND FRATERNITÉ

lower classes and prevent outright revolution, King Louis XVI assembled the Estates-General—a protodemocratic body comprised of members of the clergy, nobility, and the bourgeoisie—and invited its representatives to present their grievances to the court. Unfortunately, and perhaps unavoidably, dissent among the three orders of the Estates-General devolved into arguments and stagnation. As a result the nonaristocratic Third Estate—which represented a hugely disproportionate majority of the country's population—began to mobilize independently to support their goals of equal representation and direct representation.

In June 1789, fearing that they would be overruled by the two privileged orders in any attempt at reform, the deputies of the Third Estate led in the formation of the revolutionary National Assembly. The creation of the National Assembly signalled the end of representation based on the traditional social classes. The new organization gathered at an indoor tennis court and vowed not to leave until they had created a constitution for a new France. Despite their initial resistance, the majority of the noble members of the Estates-General ultimately joined the National Assembly, and Louis XVI was forced to recognize the new political body, albeit reluctantly.

As a precautionary measure, the king ordered 20,000 royal troops to Paris. Publicly he justified the presence of the additional troops, claiming they were needed to protect the proceedings of the National Assembly. However many Parisians felt that the troops had been mobilized to maintain the status quo. The heightened military presence in the capital quickly pushed tensions to a breaking point. July 14 became the fateful day that thousands of patriots and revolutionaries stormed the Bastille. Finally the Revolution had come to a head.

INTRODUCTION

When news of the violent events in Paris spread to the countryside, peasants across France took up arms in their own communities. The country was ravaged by attacks on the castles of nobility, and peasants burned the contracts of their feudal obligations. This period of violent anarchy came to be known as the Great Fear, and it inspired the National Assembly to declare the abolition of feudalism.

On August 4, the National Assembly announced the declaration of the Rights of Man and of the Citizen, a revolutionary document that signalled the official death of the ancien régime. The declaration proclaimed the inalienable rights of French citizens, including the freedom of speech, a representative government, and popular sovereignty. It transformed the beliefs of the Enlightenment into political and social reality and became an inspiration for later documents of a similar nature (including the United States' Bill of Rights, written two years later in 1791).

While the declaration established an essential foundation for the new society, a constitution was still needed to develop a functional legal system. Drafting this document would prove to be a much greater challenge. The Assembly had to grapple with questions of representation: How would delegates by elected? What place would the king retain (if any) within the new system of government? And—an issue of utmost importance—what role would the church play in the new French government? On September 3, 1791, the National Assembly presented a final version of their new constitution, but the document's moderate tone left many radical patriots such as Maximilien de Robespierre unsatisfied.

In the spring of 1792 terror returned to France, both at home and abroad. The Legislative Assembly declared war on

THE FRENCH REVOLUTION, NAPOLEON, AND THE REPUBLIC:
LIBERTÉ, ÉGALITÉ, AND FRATERNITÉ

Austria and Prussia based on the belief that those countries were harbouring a great number of French émigrés who had fled during the unrest and plotted against the Revolutionary government. Prussia quickly responded by announcing its intent to help reinstate the monarchy in Paris and mobilizing troops toward the capital. Spain, Piedmont, and Britain quickly joined Austria and Prussia, leaving the French army spread thin across five fronts.

To intensify matters, in August of that year a Jacobin extremist group led by Robespierre laid siege to the Tuileries Palace and captured Louis XVI. The Jacobins forcibly replaced the newly formed Legislative Assembly with the more radical National Convention. The disgraced former king was sent to the guillotine—an instrument used to decapitate a person by means of a heavy blade—with the rest of the royal family soon to follow.

Louis XVI's beheading marks the beginning of the Second Revolution. Recurring grain and flour shortages revealed how little had changed for the poorest members of society, as they once again could not afford basic sustenance. Uprisings began in May 1793 in Lyon and Marseille, and the Jacobin radicals became the preeminent political group in France.

The period of Jacobin rule became known as the Reign of Terror because of the mass bloodshed and violence that it brought. Aristocrats and political dissidents were sent to the guillotine in droves. The Jacobins were committed to a strict policy of capital punishment for most any offense, and local revolutionary committees were empowered to arrest any perceived offender. More than 10,000 individuals were either executed or perished in prisons in a period that was not even a full year.

While the Jacobins are best remembered for their bloody politics, they also introduced a number of essential changes to

INTRODUCTION

the evolving French political system. Perhaps most importantly, they replaced the Gregorian calendar with the modern French calendar, symbolizing a triumph of science and logic over a then-antiquated religious belief system. However, the extreme violence and aggression of Jacobin rule made their reign unsustainable. With the death of Robespierre in July 1794, power shifted to more moderate groups, ushering in a period known as the Thermidorian Reaction.

A new constitution was drafted that created a bicameral legislature, emergency powers to restrict the freedom of the press, and a new tax system. Economic regulations were dismantled in favour of free-trade principles, and a certain amount of order was restored. (Although, in spite of the reforms, the majority of the nation's power and wealth remained relatively centralized, and peasants still struggled to afford basic necessities such as flour. Such "luxury" items as fuel, dairy, meat, and even soap were still reserved for only the elite members of society.)

Much of the relative peace that France finally seemed to find was due in large part to an ambitious general named Napoleon Bonaparte. Through a successful coup d'état in 1799, Napoleon seized political power and established an impressive political regime known as the Consulate. His rule was defined primarily by the reconcentration of power in the executive branch, however, he was widely supported by the French population who saw in him the potential for a brighter future. The citizens of France were exhausted and traumatized after years of political turmoil and violence. Napoleon represented a return to order.

Under Napoleonic rule, the press, which had grown increasingly powerful throughout the Revolution, was heavily censored. Simultaneously, Napoleon established the foundations of the modern police state, characterized by

THE FRENCH REVOLUTION, NAPOLEON, AND THE REPUBLIC:
LIBERTÉ, ÉGALITÉ, AND FRATERNITÉ

More than a man of the Revolution, Napoleon Bonaparte was a man of the 18th century and the last of the era's so-called enlightened despots. He consolidated power in the executive branch and returned France to order after years of revolutionary political upheaval.

INTRODUCTION

increased public surveillance. These elements, paired with the implementation of a civil code known as the Napoleonic Code, would come to form the basis of modern French society.

Napoleon also successfully reintegrated the Roman Catholic church into both the economy and social order of France. Motivated not by religious fervour, but rather the desire to bring the church clearly under the authority of the state, Napoleon was ultimately able to establish the church as yet another institution through which he could exert governmental power.

In 1804 France entered into a period of aggressive warfare and conquest. Under Napoleon's military leadership France would end up expanding its empire to include Holland, Tuscany, Piedmont, Genoa, and the Rhineland. The emperor's hunger for complete conquest of Europe led him to begin a misguided attack on Russia with the intention of humbling what he called "the colossus of Northern barbarism." This venture would cost him almost two-thirds of his troops, and after a number of subsequent failed battles, Prussian forces decisively defeated Napoleon at the Battle of Waterloo.

The French Revolution and the Napoleonic era formed not only the basis of modern French society but of modernity itself. To this day the French Revolution represents one of the most defining moments in political history. In toppling the aristocracy, the revolutionaries ushered in not only a new form of government, but also a new era defined by logic, science, and reason. Although in some respects Napoleon's France represented a return to the consolidation of power that defined the ancien régime, the underlying social order had been radically restructured: the Roman Catholic Church had been domesticated by the state; inherited status replaced

THE FRENCH REVOLUTION, NAPOLEON, AND THE REPUBLIC:
LIBERTÉ, EGALITÉ, AND FRATERNITÉ

by a meritocracy; and constitutionally defined rights granted to all citizens.

In the context of political revolutions, the French Revolution stands out as the goals of the revolutionaries far exceeded a desire to simply overthrow the existing government; the citizens of France sought to impose a new understanding of human nature and society itself. The decapitation of King Louis XVI was not only a practical—and political—necessity, but also a symbolic act that divorced power from divinity and demonstrated the might of the masses.

History has proven that such fervour can be difficult to contain. In his attempt to bring the entirety of Europe under French dominance, Napoleon ended up spreading the fundamental principles of the French Revolution. For instance his occupation of Spain in 1808 was one of the sparks that ignited the revolutionary movements in Latin America that would lead to their almost entire independence by 1826.

In the 21st century we continue to see echoes of the French Revolution in such populist movements as the Arab Spring begun in 2010 and the Occupy Wall Street protests of 2011. In fact, wherever citizens rise up against perceived tyranny, oppression, and inequality, glimpses of the 18th-century French revolutionary fervour can be seen. Like other revolutions of the period, it was a movement destined to have lasting effects in the way it altered our understanding of the nature of government and citizenship. Not only does this resource provide a comprehensive account of the causes, events, and consequences of the French Revolution, but it also handles the important task of situating the revolution within its larger historical and global context.

CHAPTER 1

PREREVOLUTIONARY FRANCE

The year 1789 is the great dividing line in the history of modern France. The fall of the Bastille, a medieval fortress used as a state prison, on July 14, 1789, symbolizes for France, as well as for other nations, the end of the premodern era characterized by an organicist and religiously sanctioned traditionalism. With the French Revolution began the institutionalization of secularized individualism in both social life and politics; individualism and rationality found expression in parliamentary government and written constitutionalism. Obviously, the English and American revolutions of 1688 and 1776 prefigure these changes, but it was the more universalist French Revolution that placed individualism and rationality squarely at the centre of human concerns.

Because the revolutionary events had such earthshaking power, the history of France in the century preceding 1789 has until recently been seen as a long prologue to the coming drama, a period marked by the decay of the ancien régime ("old regime"), a locution created during the Revolution. Some contemporary historians, however, reject this view and present 18th-century France as

THE FRENCH REVOLUTION, NAPOLEON, AND THE REPUBLIC:
LIBERTÉ, ÉGALITÉ, AND FRATERNITÉ

a society undergoing rapid but manageable social, economic, and cultural change. They perceive the French Revolution as a political event that could have been avoided if the French monarchy had been more consistent in its effort to modify political institutions in order to keep up with the new needs of its people.

SOCIAL AND POLITICAL HERITAGE

To understand the developments of the 18th century and to follow the scholarly debates, one may begin with a definition of the ancien régime. Its essence lay in the interweaving of the state's social, political, and economic forms; the term itself, though primarily a political concept, has also always had a clear social and economic resonance.

In the society of the ancien régime, all men and women were, by birth, subjects as well as members of an estate and province. The king was viewed as a fatherly figure who ruled by divine right. All rights and status flowed from the social institutions, which were divided into three orders: clergy, nobility, and others (the Third Estate). There was no national citizenship.

THE SOCIAL ORDER OF THE ANCIEN RÉGIME

Under the ancien régime, the lives of French men and women of all ranks and estates took shape within a number of overlapping institutions, each with rules that entitled its members to enjoy particular privileges (a term derived from the Latin words for "private law"). Rights and status flowed as a rule from the group to the individual rather than from individuals to the group, as was true after 1789.

France itself can be conceived of as an aggregate of differentiated groups or communities (villages, parishes, or guilds), all of them theoretically comparable but all of them different. In many respects the kingdom was an assembly of varying provinces, a number of them endowed with vestigial representative institutions. In some important ways France was not truly a unit of government. Unlike England, for example, France was not a single customs union; more tariffs had to be paid by shippers on brandy floated down the Garonne to Bordeaux than on wine shipped from France to Britain.

The concept of national citizenship was not unknown in France under the ancien régime, existing in the sense that all Frenchmen, regardless of their rank and privileges, had certain legal rights denied to all foreigners. There was, however, no French nation whose citizens taken one by one were equal before man-made law, as was true after 1789. Laws were in the main inherited, not made.

This is not to say that France, though structured around the "premodern" concept of the guild, or group, or corps, was a static or, materially speaking, a stable society. For many artisans, peregrination was a way of life, and many years of their young manhood were spent on a *tour de France*, which took them from city to city in order to learn their trade. Serfdom was practically unknown (only 140,000 serfs remained in France in 1789, none of them on crown lands, where Jacques Necker, the comptroller general, had abolished serfdom in 1779), and peasants were free to move as they wished from one village to

THE FRENCH REVOLUTION, NAPOLEON, AND THE REPUBLIC:
LIBERTÉ, ÉGALITÉ, AND FRATERNITÉ

The historical provinces of France (before 1789).

the next. Indeed, such large numbers of people were moving around that the fear of unattached vagrants was strong in pre-revolutionary France.

PREREVOLUTIONARY FRANCE

MONARCHY AND CHURCH

In the 18th century, justifications of royal authority drew on many traditions. The king still claimed the status of a feudal suzerain of his subjects. Familial imagery was an important component of royal rhetoric; the king of France was father of his subjects. His right to reign echoed all husbands' right to rule over their wives and all fathers' right to rule over their children. His messages, however draconian and confiscatory they might be, were invariably couched in a rhetoric of religious and paternal solicitude.

The king, moreover, was a Christian monarch and as such was endowed with quasi-priestly functions. He was anointed at his coronation with holy chrism said to have been brought from heaven by a dove. It was thought that, as evidence of his special status, he could cure scrofula by his touch. The relationship of church and state was complex. Oftentimes the king did not hesitate to exploit the church, over which he held extensive power by virtue of the still-valid Concordat of Bologna of 1516. Monarchs used their right to appoint bishops and abbots to secure the loyalty of impoverished or ambitious nobles. The crown asserted its right to regulate church policies, limit the authority of the pope over French Catholics, and abolish or consolidate monastic orders.

Nonetheless, until 1788 the Roman Catholic Church retained in France unusually broad doctrinal rights and social prestige, even by the standards prevailing in central or southern Europe, not to speak of what held true in the far more tolerant countries of northern Europe (Prussia, Holland, and Britain). French Protestants were denied religious toleration until 1787. Jews were tolerated only as quasi foreigners until 1791. Of considerable symbolic importance was the fact that

THE FRENCH REVOLUTION, NAPOLEON, AND THE REPUBLIC:
LIBERTÉ, ÉGALITÉ, AND FRATERNITÉ

before 1789 it was the church that kept the registers of births and deaths that marked the beginning and end of each person's earthly existence. The church, the police, and the courts collaborated closely to maintain the prestige of religion; until at least the 1780s the church severely condemned licentious or irreligious books such as Rousseau's *Émile*, which was burned in 1762 by order of the Parlement of Paris, a measure that did little to stop its circulation.

The monarchy basically respected the various rights of the Church accrued by tradition, as it did the civil and property rights, or "liberties," of its subjects generally. Continuity ordinarily seemed to be the first principle of the French state, and it was inherent in the concept of the king itself: the king was held to have two bodies, a physical one, which necessarily decayed, and a spiritual one, which never died. In this view, the main purpose of the French state was to defend vested interests—i.e., to maintain continuity rather than to change the existing order.

COMMITMENT TO MODERNIZATION

The great peculiarity of the ancien régime was that a system committed to preserving tradition also contained within it powerful forces for change. The absolute monarchy had been developed between 1624 and 1642 at the hands of a series of powerful ministers and secretaries under both Louis XIII and Louis XIV. Primary among them was Armand-Jean du Plessis, cardinal and duke de Richelieu and chief minister to Louis XIII. His early work was later followed by Cardinal Jules Mazarin (first minister of France following Richelieu's death), Jean-Baptiste Colbert (controller general of finance and then secretary of state for the navy under Louis XIV), and François-Michel Le Tellier (secretary of state for war, also

Portrait of Cardinal de Richelieu by Baroque painter Philippe de Champaigne. It is in the Museum of Fine Arts in Strasbourg, France.

under Louis XIV). Their consolidation of the power of the monarchy was guided by a modern raison d'état, in which the state was eager to further changes of all kinds for its own purposes. Administratively, its absolutist will, formulated at Versailles in a complex array of governmental councils, was enforced in the provinces by the intendants and their subordinates. The monarchy favoured modern manufacturing and, more desultorily, modern finance. It protected and firmly guided intellectuals through the Académie

THE FRENCH REVOLUTION, NAPOLEON, AND THE REPUBLIC:
LIBERTÉ, ÉGALITÉ, AND FRATERNITÉ

Française. With greater hesitation, the monarchy also promoted France's drive to obtain economic and military supremacy not just in Europe but overseas as well, in North America, India, Africa, and the Caribbean.

Divided in its goals, some of them traditional and others modern, the state was also ideologically double minded. In the 17th century many intellectuals (some of them clerics such as Bishop Jacques-Bénigne Bossuet [1627–1704]) developed a Hobbesian justification of absolutist rule, which was renewed throughout the 18th century. Religion and tradition went hand in hand, but absolutist theoreticians went further. They justified the state's right not only to legislate and tax more or less at will but also to imprison arbitrarily without due process of law. The lettres de cachet, which allowed the king to have individuals committed to the Bastille and to other prisons forever and without any kind of trial, were seldom given out, but when they were, they usually went to fathers who wished to correct their wayward children. But they did exist, as liberal or scurrilous propagandists knew full well, sometimes first-hand: about one-fourth of the 5,279 people imprisoned in the Bastille between 1660 and 1790 were connected with the world of the book. Royal proclamations often stressed, however, the king's obligation to govern in the interests of his people. The *parlements*, frequent

LETTRES DE CACHET

Lettres de cachet (French: "letters of the sign [or signet]") were letters signed by the king of France and countersigned by a secretary of state and used primarily to authorize someone's imprisonment.

It was an important instrument of administration under the ancien régime. However lettres de cachet were greatly abused during the 17th and 18th centuries, making them the subject of numerous complaints in the early days of the Revolution.

State lettres de cachet were sent by the government in the interests of society, either to maintain public order or to assure the proper functioning of institutions. In the first case, a public authority might obtain from the king the orders for someone's detention for a limited period of time, or a public prosecutor would demand a lettre de cachet for the arrest of an accused person before trial. In the second case, the king might use a lettre de cachet to summon political bodies (such as the Estates-General), to order them to discuss a particular matter or to exclude from their meetings some person or persons considered undesirable. Lettres de cachet were also used to arrest suspect foreigners or spies. They were also granted to private persons for action on another individual. Couched in very brief, direct terms, a lettre de cachet simply commanded the recipient to obey the orders therein without delay, giving no explanation.

The effect of a lettre de cachet was to initiate and enforce the imprisonment of an individual in a state fortress, particularly the Bastille, or in a convent or hospital. That the duration of the imprisonment was not necessarily specified in the lettre de cachet served to aggravate the arbitrary character of the measure taken. Nor was there any legal mechanism for appeal against a lettre de cachet; release, no less than detention, depended entirely upon the king's pleasure. In the law of the ancien régime, the lettre de cachet was thus an expression of that exercise of justice that the king reserved to himself, independently of the law courts and their processes, just as he reserved the right to grant *lettres de grâce*, or pardons, to persons who had been convicted by the courts.

The use of lettres de cachet would later be abolished by the Constituent Assembly in March 1790.

THE FRENCH REVOLUTION, NAPOLEON, AND THE REPUBLIC:
LIBERTÉ, ÉGALITÉ, AND FRATERNITÉ

critics of arbitrary rule, spread the notion that subjects' rights were protected by a fixed, if ill-defined, constitution that could not be altered without the consent of their representatives.

CONTINUITY AND CHANGE

The political history of 18th-century France can be conceptualized in terms of the double heritage and the problems it entailed. The discussion may be linked to two issues: first, the economic transformation of a traditional and essentially agricultural society by both commerce and ideas; and, second, the state's efforts (and eventual inability) to modernize and unify its structure and purpose to encompass the changed economic and cultural expectations of the nation's elites.

In contrast to the France of Louis XIV's *grand siècle* ("great century"), beset by economic stagnation and periodic food shortages, 18th-century France enjoyed a climate of growing prosperity, fueled in part by a sustained rise in population. The kingdom's population, which had barely grown at all during the years 1500 to 1700, increased from approximately 20 million at the end of Louis XIV's reign to about 28 million by 1789. Better preventive medicine, a decline in infant mortality, and the near disappearance of widespread famine after 1709 all served to increase the population. Birth rates continued to be very high, despite both a traditional pattern of late marriage (men on the average at age 27, women at 24 or 25) and the beginnings of the practice of birth control, the effect of which was to become evident only after the Revolution. The yearly number of deaths per 10,000 fell from about 400 in 1750 to 350 in 1775, 328 in 1790, and 298 in 1800. The increased population meant more mouths to feed but also more consumers, more workers seeking employment, and more opportunities for investment; in short, every aspect of French life was affected.

AGRICULTURAL PATTERNS

In its basic organization, French agriculture continued its age-old patterns. This contrasted starkly with England, where new agricultural techniques as well as major changes in the control of land—convertible husbandry (a progressive form of land use that did away with the wasteful fallowing of land every two or three years) and the enclosure movement (which made possible the consolidation of small parcels of land into large farms fenced off from use by the rest of the community)—were beginning to cause an agricultural revolution. In France there was no significant enclosure movement, despite enabling legislation that allowed the division of some common lands in 1767 and again in 1773. Communal patterns of planting—very common in northern France, where a three-field system ordinarily prevailed—were not suspended. Modest improvements in farming techniques and the introduction of new crops such as corn (maize) and potatoes allowed French farms to feed the country's growing population. The increased number of peasants led to further subdivision of land and greater competition for leases; the economic benefits of agricultural growth went mostly to landlords and the small minority of prosperous peasants. In fact, the economic status of many peasants deteriorated markedly in the 18th century; perhaps as many as one-third of them were sporadically indigent, though there was no decline in the peasants' share of the land. In 1789 French peasants still

THE FRENCH REVOLUTION, NAPOLEON, AND THE REPUBLIC:
LIBERTÉ, ÉGALITÉ, AND FRATERNITÉ

owned about one-third of the arable land, most of it in small plots of less than 10 acres (4 hectares); nobles owned about one-fifth of the land, the church one-sixth, and bourgeois landlords about one-third.

INDUSTRIAL PRODUCTION

After 1740 industrial production in France rose annually by about 2 percent overall and even more in some sectors. During the later decades of the 18th century, French industrial production grew rapidly, although not on the same scale as in Britain, whose industrial development had begun 60 years before that of the French. Coal mining was a major industry by 1789, its production nearly 6 percent higher in the 1780s than in the preceding decade. Mining attracted vast amounts of capital, some of it from the aristocracy. In 1789 the Mines d'Anzin near the Belgian border already employed thousands of workers. In textiles, entrepreneurs such as the Swiss Protestant Guillaume-Philippe Oberkampf created new manufactories that permitted better regulation and control of production. Most production continued to be centred in small artisanal workshops, however, and power-driven machinery remained a rarity.

Although transportation difficulties and internal customs barriers meant that France on the eve of the Revolution was not yet a unified national market (as Britain had long since been), price discrepancies from province to province, as well as between northern and southern France, were less significant than before. Throughout the country the demand rose for urban manufactured goods and for those luxury

PREREVOLUTIONARY FRANCE

FRENCH SHIP DESIGN WAS JUST ONE EXAMPLE OF SUPERIOR FRENCH PRODUCTION IN THE 18TH CENTURY. ILLUSTRATED IN THIS WATERCOLOR IS L'ASTRÉE, A FRENCH FRIGATE IN USE 1786–90, PAINTED BY FRANÇOIS ROUX ABOUT 1825.

items (textiles, porcelains, furniture, *articles de Paris*) that the French excelled in producing before 1800. French engineers and artisans were highly skilled. French ship design, for example, was superior to that of the English, who routinely copied captured French men-of-war. George Washington, the president of the United States, wishing to buy the best watch available anywhere, turned to the American minister in Paris because the world's most accurate timepieces were still made in France.

THE FRENCH REVOLUTION, NAPOLEON, AND THE REPUBLIC:
LIBERTÉ, ÉGALITÉ, AND FRATERNITÉ

ILLUSTRATED IN THIS 18TH-CENTURY ENGRAVING IS FORT-DE-FRANCE, MARTINIQUE. MARTINIQUE ALONG WITH GUADELOUPE AND SAINT-DOMINGUE (MODERN-DAY HAITI) MADE UP THE FRENCH COLONIAL HOLDINGS IN THE CARIBBEAN, THE SO-CALLED SUGAR ISLANDS THAT CONTRIBUTED TO THE ANCIEN RÉGIME'S WEALTH.

COMMERCE

Commerce, especially with the colonies, was an important area of change as well. France's first colonial empire, essentially located in North America, was a source of great wealth. Even though France lost both Canada and India during the Seven Years' War (1756–63), the Caribbean sugar islands continued to be the most lucrative source of French colonial activity in the last 100 years of the ancien régime. The French shared the West Indies with Spain and England: Cuba, Puerto Rico, and the eastern half of Hispaniola belonged to Spain; Jamaica belonged to England; but Guadeloupe, Martinique, and Saint-Domingue (Haiti)—the richest of all nonwhite 18th-century colonies in the world—were French. In Saint-Domingue 30,000 whites stood an uneasy watch over a black slave population that grew to more than 400,000 by 1789. In the islands, the slaves produced sugarcane and coffee, which were refined in France at Nantes, Rochefort, and Bordeaux and often reexported to central and northern Europe. This triangular trade grew 10-fold between 1715 and 1789, and the value of international exports in the 1780s amounted to nearly one-fourth of national income. The sugar trade enriched the planters, the bankers in Paris who had acted as brokers for import and reexport, and the manufacturers of luxury goods that were shipped from France to the Caribbean. Not surprisingly, the French colonial trade was a closely watched process, governed by mercantilist protective tariffs and rules.

Indirectly millions of Frenchmen were affected by the accelerating tempo of economic life. The circulation of gold specie in the kingdom as a whole rose from 731 million livres in 1715 to some 2 billion livres in 1788. Domestic commerce also expanded in the 18th century. The urban population and even prosperous peasants began to acquire a taste for new luxuries. Estate inventories show that even modest households were buying more varied clothing, a wider range of furniture, kitchen articles, books, and other items their ancestors could not have afforded. By the early 1780s more than 40 regional newspapers with advertising, or *affiches*, had been founded, a clear sign that France was becoming a consumer society.

THE FRENCH REVOLUTION, NAPOLEON, AND THE REPUBLIC:
LIBERTÉ, ÉGALITÉ, AND FRATERNITÉ

CITIES

Commerce rather than industry buoyed up French cities, especially the Atlantic seaports. In 1789, 15 percent of Frenchmen lived in cities with more than 2,000 inhabitants. Still, Paris, a city of about 600,000 inhabitants, was only half the size of London, the world's largest seaport. But, regardless of their size, French cities were centres of intellectual transformation. It was there, in the Sociétés de Pensées, Masonic lodges, and some 32 provincial academies, that writers found their public. There also took place the cultural revolution that inspired the writers in turn and the economic changes that gave momentum to the cultural upheaval.

CULTURAL TRANSFORMATION

The industrial and commercial developments, already significant by themselves, were the cause, and perhaps also the effect, of a wider and still more momentous change preceding the Revolution—the Enlightenment. Today the Enlightenment can be understood as the conscious formulation of a profound cultural transformation. Epistemologically, the French Enlightenment relied on three sources: rationalism, which had in France a strong tradition dating to Descartes; empiricism, which was borrowed from English thought and which in France underpinned the work of such writers as Claude-Adrien Helvétius (1715–71), Paul-Henri Dietrich, baron d'Holbach (1723–89), Étienne Bonnot de Condillac (1715–80), and Julien Offroy de La Mettrie (1709–51), the author of a book eloquently entitled *L'Homme machine* (1747;

Man a Machine); and an amorphous concept of nature that was particularly strong in the immensely popular and important work of Jean-Jacques Rousseau (1712–78) and, in the 1780s, in the works of widely read pre-Romantic writers such as Jacques-Henri Bernardin de Saint-Pierre (1737–1814). The relationship between these intellectual developments and the Revolution of 1789 remains a subject of dispute among historians, but there is no doubt that Enlightenment critiques undermined belief in the traditional institutions that the Revolutionary movement was to destroy.

Though far apart from one another in a strict philosophical sense, these sources of inspiration generated a number of shared beliefs that were of obvious political consequence. The enlightened subjects of Louis XV and Louis XVI were increasingly convinced that French institutions of government and justice could be radically improved. Tradition seemed to them an increasingly inadequate principle to follow in such matters. Meliorism, gauged especially by the progress of the sciences, was one of the

THE PHILOSOPHICAL INFLUENCE OF SUCH ENLIGHTENMENT AUTHORS AS MONTESQUIEU, JEAN-JACQUES ROUSSEAU, AND VOLTAIRE (PORTRAYED HERE) CONTRIBUTED TO THE PRE-REVOLUTIONARY CULTURAL TRANSFORMATION IN FRANCE.

THE FRENCH REVOLUTION, NAPOLEON, AND THE REPUBLIC:
LIBERTÉ, ÉGALITÉ, AND FRATERNITÉ

cardinal beliefs of the age. Regarding the economy, physiocrats such as the king's own doctor, François Quesnay (1694–1774), praised the virtue of free-market economics and, as they put it, of *laissez-faire, laissez-aller* ("allow to do, allow to go"). The Encyclopédistes—the contributors to the great *Encyclopédie* edited by Denis Diderot (1713–84)—spread the idea that agricultural and manufacturing processes could be rationally analyzed and improved; the work also criticized religious and political orthodoxy. Voltaire (1694–1778), the most celebrated French Enlightenment author, used his sharp wit to skewer the absurdities of absolutism and intolerance. His eloquent defense of the Protestant merchant Jean Calas, broken on the wheel in 1762 for the supposed murder of his suicidal son, made him the model of the engaged intellectual, rallying public opinion against injustice.

THE INFLUENCE OF MONTESQUIEU AND ROUSSEAU

Two Enlightenment authors who had an especially profound impact on the future revolutionaries were Charles-Louis de Secondat, baron de La Brède et de Montesquieu (1689–1755), and Jean-Jacques Rousseau (1712–78). In his *Lettres persanes* (1721; *Persian Letters*), Montesquieu, a wealthy aristocratic member of the Parlement of Bordeaux, used the device of a foreign visitor to highlight the contradictions of the government shortly after the death of Louis XIV. His daring jabs at the pope, "an ancient idol, worshiped now from habit," and at Catholic doctrine brought down the wrath of the authorities but did nothing to stop the book's success. Written in an entertaining and accessible style, the *Persian Letters* did not present a clear set of doctrines: instead, readers were drawn into a process of dialogue and critique modeled by the novel's characters. In his masterwork, *De l'esprit des loix* (1748; *The Spirit of the Laws*), Montesquieu presented a survey of political institutions throughout the world. Drawing on both the rationalist and empiricist traditions, he analyzed politics in purely secular terms, arguing that each country's laws developed in response to its climate and the nature of its customs. His comparative approach made it clear that, in his view, no political system could claim divine sanction. His personal sympathies lay with mixed forms of government, in which a separation of powers protected individual liberties; his description of the English constitution, in which the king shared power with Parliament, strongly influenced French political thinking. A former *parlementaire* himself, Montesquieu argued that the aristocratic courts were "intermediary bodies," whose resistance to royal authority prevented abuses. Although he was himself no revolutionary, his ideas had great influence at the beginning of the revolutionary movement in 1789; in the Revolution's early phase, he was cited more often than any other authority.

A generation younger than Montesquieu, Rousseau raised profound questions about both private and public life. According to Rousseau, the self becomes empowered in private union with the beloved other, as portrayed in his immensely popular novel *Julie; ou, la nouvelle Héloïse* (1761; *Julie; or, the New Eloise*), or in public union with one's fraternally minded fellow citizens, as explained in *Du contrat social* (1762; *The Social Contract*), a work less widely read before 1789 but even more symptomatic of change.

Rousseau argued for a reconstruction of private and domestic as well as public life, to make both more in accord with human nature. Women, he claimed, have a natural

THE FRENCH REVOLUTION, NAPOLEON, AND THE REPUBLIC:
LIBERTÉ, ÉGALITÉ, AND FRATERNITÉ

Illustration of Émile from Émile; or, on Education (1762), by Jean-Jacques Rousseau.

vocation to be wives and mothers; they are to leave public affairs to men. He put forward the harmonious domestic family as a new cultural ideal and stigmatized ancien régime society, with its emphasis on fashion and its influential "public women," such as royal mistresses and the salon hostesses who played a critical role in promoting the Enlightenment. Rousseau's insistence that mothers should breast-feed their children clashed with the realities of French life, where the employment of wet nurses was more common than in any other European country and symbolized his program for a more "natural" style of life.

Rousseau's second best-selling novel, *Émile; ou, de l'éducation* (1762; *Émile; or, on Education*), illustrated how children could be educated to lead a "natural" life. Its most controversial chapter, the "Profession of Faith of a Savoyard Vicar," suggested that nature alone provided humanity with the religious knowledge it needed; this dismissal of the church and the Bible naturally led to the book's condemnation. Rousseau's concern for education was part of a wider movement.

The French administrator, reformer, and economist Anne-Robert-Jacques Turgot, baron de l'Aulne (1712–81), expressed the new sensibility when he wrote that the education of children was the basis of national unity and mores.

In 1763 a prominent *parlementaire* named La Chalotais even put forward a scheme for lay and national primary education. An important landmark in this respect was the expulsion from France in 1764 of the Jesuits, who had theretofore dominated French secondary education. Increasingly, the French language was substituted for Latin in the secondary schools, or *collèges* (the forerunners of today's lycées). Rhetoric gave way to an emphasis on more "natural" manners and modes of expression. History was raised to the level of a serious discipline; with Voltaire's *Le Siècle de Louis XIV* (1751; *The Age of Louis XIV*), modern French historiography began, and there were echoes of this new attitude in the programs of the secondary schools, which added mathematics, physics, and geography to their curricula.

Rousseau developed the political consequences of his thought in his *Social Contract* (1762). Because men are by nature free, Rousseau argued, the only natural and legitimate polity is one in which all members are citizens with equal rights and have the ability to participate in making the laws under which they live. Like Montesquieu, Rousseau himself was no revolutionary; he expressed a deep pessimism about the chances of freeing humanity from the corrupting institutions that were in place. Although his theories did influence critics of the French monarchy even before 1789, they achieved an unanticipated relevance during the Revolution, especially during

THE FRENCH REVOLUTION, NAPOLEON, AND THE REPUBLIC:
LIBERTÉ, ÉGALITÉ, AND FRATERNITÉ

its radical phase when Rousseau was read as an advocate of Jacobin-style democracy.

Exposure to such writers as Diderot, Guillaume-Thomas, abbé de Raynal (1713–96), author of the anticolonialist *Histoire des deux Indes* (1770; History of the two Indies), and Jean-Jacques Barthélemy (1716–95); to such painters as Jacques-Louis David (1748–1825) and Joseph-Marie Vien (1716–1809); to such musicians as Christoph Gluck (1714–87); and to such visionary architects as Claude-Nicolas Ledoux (1736–1806) and Étienne-Louis Boullée (1728–99) enabled the educated public of the 1770s and '80s to pursue and sharpen their new insights. It allowed them to explore the limits of the private domain as well as to clarify their new understanding of the public good. These radical ideas had transforming power. Rousseau's message especially appealed to the deeper instincts of his contemporaries, inspiring them with a quasi-utopian view of what might be done in this world.

The ideological or cultural transformation was in some ways limited to a narrow segment of society. In 1789 only one-third of the population, living for the most part in northern and eastern France, could both read and write French. (Outside the aristocracy and upper bourgeoisie, literacy for women was considerably below that of men.) About one-third of the king's subjects could not even speak French. Nonetheless, even though probably not much more than half a million people were directly involved in the cultural upheaval, their influence was decisive.

The concerns of the new "high culture" were intensely personal and, for that reason, deeply felt, even by people who did not participate in it directly. Readers of sentimental prose might after all also be employers, husbands, and fathers, who would treat their dependents differently. Printed materials were certainly more widely available in the 18th century than ever before, and new ideas reached a wide public, even if often only in watered-down form. Newspapers, some of them from abroad, were widely read (and manipulated by the royal government to influence opinion). Many pamphleteers were ready to be hired by whoever had money to pay for their services. Lawyers published their briefs. Theatrical performances, such as Pierre-Augustin Caron de Beaumarchais's comedy *Le Mariage de Figaro* (1784; *The Marriage of Figaro*), which openly exposed aristocratic privilege, were widely publicized events. In the 1780s censorship was increasingly desultory. Public opinion, whose verdict was identified by the middle class not with the expression of its own particular desires but as the voice of universal common sense and reason, became a tribunal of ideological appeal, an intellectual court of last resort, to which even the monarchy instinctively appealed.

These sweeping changes had created a country that by 1788 was deeply divided ideologically and economically. The salons of Paris, many of them directed by women, were the worldwide focus of a rationalist and Deist Enlightenment; both Catherine the Great and Thomas Jefferson, though far removed from each other in most respects, shared an abiding interest in the latest intellectual fashions from Paris. But, whatever held true for influential circles, most Frenchmen in these same years remained deeply religious, certainly in the provinces but possibly in Paris as well. Most of the books and pictures Parisians bought on the eve of the Revolution were still related to religious themes. The country was also divided economically; whereas France's foreign trade was very lively, most of the rural communities were, by English standards, unproductive and immobile villages.

CAUSES OF THE REVOLUTION

In broad terms, 18th-century French politics could be defined as the response of the monarchic state to the emergence of the new cultural and economic configurations that had transformed the lives and especially the imaginations of French men and women. The question was whether the Bourbon monarchy could rationalize its administration and find a way to adapt itself in the 1770s and '80s to the new perception of the relationship between citizen and state as it had come to be defined by the changes that characterized the period.

On the issue of political mutation, historical opinion is divided. One set of discussions revolves around the issue of whether the monarchy's efforts at reform were sufficient; whereas some historians believe that the ancien régime almost succeeded, first in the 1770s and once again in the early 1780s, others argue more pessimistically that the efforts of the monarchy were insubstantial. A more radical view, by contrast, holds that the extent of reform was irrelevant because no monarch, however brilliant, could have met the rising liberal and nationalist expectations of tens of thousands of dissatisfied and vocal people, steeped in Enlightenment thought, who were committed to becoming the empowered citizens of a fraternal state.

The weight of evidence appears to be that the monarchy was by the late 1780s doomed to destruction, both from its inability to carry on the absolutist, administrative work formerly accomplished by such men as Colbert and by the nature of its critics' desires; the gap separating the traditionalism of the monarchy and the ambitions of nascent public opinion was too wide.

FOREIGN POLICY AND FINANCIAL CRISIS

The 18th-century French monarchy lacked both the ambition and the means to pursue a foreign policy as far-reaching as that of Louis XIV. From the time of the War of the Spanish Succession (1701–14), when France had been invaded and nearly beaten, French statesmen pursued a double goal—the preservation of the balance of power in Europe and, in the world at large, the expansion of the French colonial empire and the containment of England. In the first decades after Louis XIV's death, French leaders sought to avoid a renewal of large-scale conflict. After 1740, when Prussia's aggressive monarch Frederick II (the Great) attacked Austria, France was drawn into a war against its traditional Habsburg foe and Vienna's ally, Britain. The end of this War of the Austrian Succession (1740–48) brought France little.

THE FRENCH REVOLUTION, NAPOLEON, AND THE REPUBLIC:
LIBERTÉ, ÉGALITÉ, AND FRATERNITÉ

THROUGHOUT THE 18TH CENTURY, FRANCE BECAME EMBROILED IN A NUMBER OF COSTLY MILITARY CONFLICTS. AMONG THESE CONFLICTS WAS THE FRENCH AND INDIAN WAR (1754-63), WHICH SAW FRANCE AND ITS TRADITIONAL FOE BRITAIN FIGHT FOR CONTROL OVER COLONIAL TERRITORY IN NORTH AMERICA. ILLUSTRATED HERE IS THE SEPTEMBER 13, 1759, BATTLE ON THE PLAINS OF ABRAHAM—A DECISIVE LOSS FOR THE FRENCH.

By 1754 France was again fighting Britain in North America. In Europe, Prussia's rapprochement with the British drove Louis XV to break tradition and ally with the Austrians in the "diplomatic revolution" of 1756, leading to the Seven Years' War. Frederick the Great's army inflicted humiliating defeats on the poorly led French armies, while the British captured French possessions in Canada, the Caribbean, and India. After the peace settlement of 1763, the foreign minister, Étienne-François, duc de Choiseul, began military reforms that laid the basis for French successes in the Revolutionary era, but France was unable to stop its Continental rivals Prussia, Austria, and Russia from seizing territory from its traditional client Poland in the First Partition of 1772.

The one French success in the century-long competition with Britain was the support given to the rebellious North American colonies in the American Revolution (1775–83). French military officers, most notably the young marquis de Lafayette, fought with the American forces, and for a short while the French navy had control of the high seas. The real victor of the Siege of Yorktown, Virginia (1781), in which the British were defeated, was less General George Washington than Admiral François-Joseph-Paul, comte de Grasse (1722–88), whose fleet had entered Chesapeake Bay. The American victory enhanced French prestige but failed to bring any territorial gains or economic advantages.

Regardless of defeat or victory, colonial and naval wars were problematic because of their prohibitive cost. In Bourbon France (as in Hanoverian England and the Prussia of the Fredericks) a high percentage of the governmental income was earmarked for war. Navies were a particularly costly commodity. The crown's inability to manage the ever-swelling deficit finally forced it to ask the country's elites for help, which, for reasons unrelated to the various wars and conflicts, they were unwilling to extend unconditionally. Money thus was a large factor in the collapse of the monarchy in 1789.

THE FRENCH REVOLUTION, NAPOLEON, AND THE REPUBLIC:
LIBERTÉ, ÉGALITÉ, AND FRATERNITÉ

Ultimately, to be sure, it was not the crown's inability to pay for wars that caused its downfall. Rather, the crown's extreme financial difficulties could have led to reforms; the need for funds might have galvanized the energies of the monarchy to carry forward the task of administrative reordering begun during the reigns of Louis XIII and Louis XIV. A more determined king might have availed himself of the problems raised by the deficit in order to overwhelm the defenders of traditionalism. In so doing, the monarchy might have satisfied enough of the desires of the Enlightenment elite to defuse the tense political situation of the late 1770s and the '80s. Although in 1789 a program of "reform from above" was no longer possible, it might well have succeeded in the early 1770s.

DOMESTIC POLICY AND REFORM EFFORTS

As stated above, in the context of 17th-century absolutism, Louis XIV had already initiated many rationalizing reforms. This statist and anticorporatist program was now embraced, but in a more liberal register, by the Enlightenment partisans of meritocratic individualism. Though Montesquieu had defended intermediary bodies such as guilds as guarantees of civic liberty, thinkers of the Enlightenment attacked them in the name of public utility and of what would later be called the rights of man. In an article written for the *Encyclopédie*, Turgot denied the sanctity of what he called foundations: "Public utility is the supreme law, and cannot be countervailed by a superstitious respect for what has been called the intents of the founders." Most foundations, he thought, had as their only purpose the satisfaction of frivolous vanity. At the other end of the social spectrum, the Protestant Rabaut Saint-Étienne, later president of the National Assembly (Assemblée Nationale), argued that "every time one creates a corporate body with privileges one creates a public enemy because a special interest is nothing else than this." No distinction was made between private interest and factional selfishness; in 1786 the future Girondin leader Jacques-Pierre Brissot was expressing what had become a commonplace when he wrote that "the history of all intermediary bodies proves, in all evidence, that to bring men and to bind men together is to develop their vices and diminish their virtues." Private benevolence applied to public purpose was loudly praised in the 1780s, and Louis XVI's finance minister, Jacques Necker (1732–1804), did a great deal for his reputation by endowing a hospital for sick children, which stands to this day. By 1789 public and charitable concern had become the themes of countless didactic works of literature and painting.

Many of the monarchy's efforts to institutionalize this new sensibility were often significant. The crown encouraged not only agriculture but also manufacturing and commerce. It allowed tax exemptions for newly cultivated land. It subsidized the slave trade, on which much of the prosperity of the Atlantic seaports was based. It improved communications and in 1747 founded the School of Bridges and Roads to train civil engineers for the royal engineering service that had existed since 1599. In the provinces, many intendants took an active role in road building and in the modernization of urban space. The crown's administrators also gave sustained thought to the abolition of internal customs and to the creation of what would have

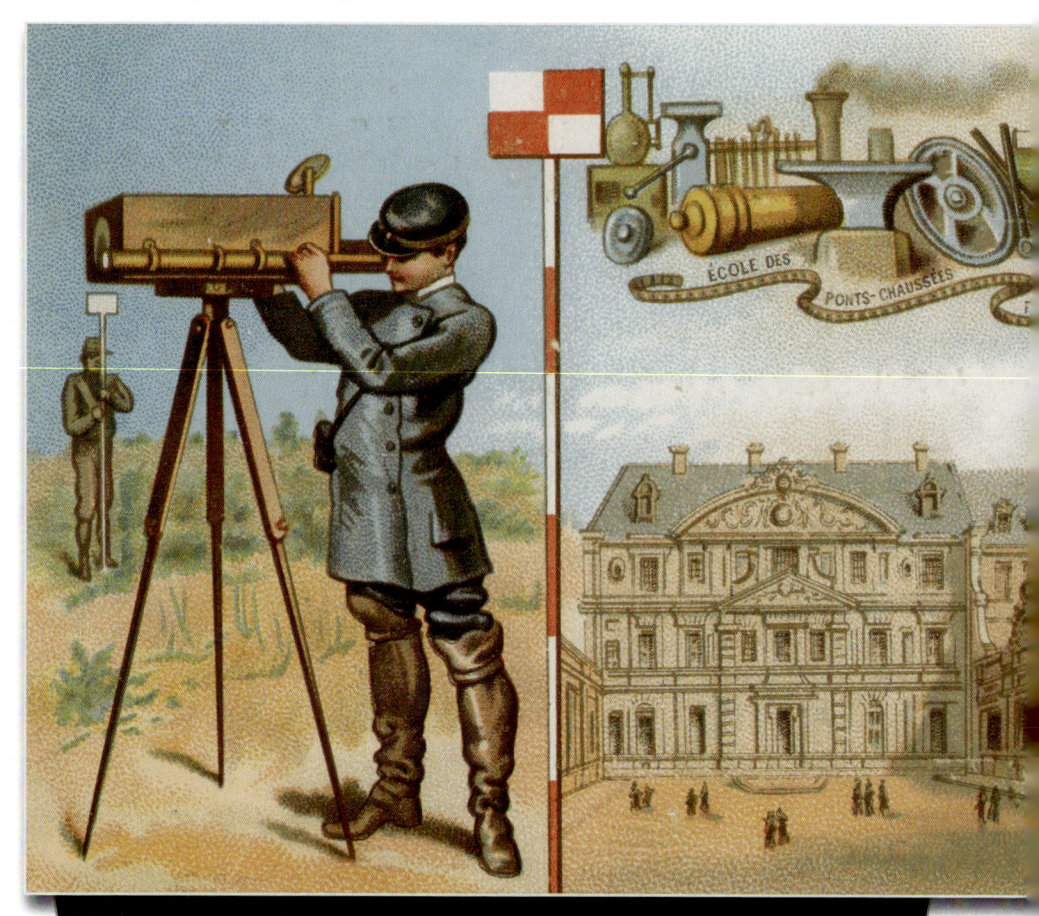

THE FRENCH REVOLUTION, NAPOLEON, AND THE REPUBLIC:
LIBERTÉ, ÉGALITÉ, AND FRATERNITÉ

This 19th-century chromolithograph illustrates the School of Bridges and Roads. The school's establishment in 1747 represents just one of the French monarchy's efforts to institutionalize modern sensibilities, particularly in the areas of agriculture, manufacturing, and commerce.

been the largest free-trade zone in Europe at the time. Social mobility was made possible; after 1750 many successful merchants and bankers were ennobled.

These were important steps. But the royal bureaucrats tried to go much further in regard to both the rationalization of the state's financial machine and the meritocratic individuation of social and economic forms.

TAX REFORM

In 1749–51 Jean-Baptiste de Machault d'Arnouville, then comptroller general of finances, tried to deal with the debts resulting from the just-concluded War of the Austrian Succession by proposing a partial reform of the tax system, his particular concern being to restrict the financial immunities of the church. In 1764 and 1765 another comptroller general, François de L'Averdy, attempted a reform of municipal representation and administration. All royal officials understood the need to reform and rationalize both the imposition and the collection of taxes; many nobles were exempted from taxation, especially in northern France, and many taxes were inefficiently collected by private tax-farmers.

The country's overall fiscal structure was highly irrational, as it had been developed by fits and starts under the goad of immediate need. There were direct taxes, some of which were collected directly by the state: the taille (a personal tax), the capitation, and the *vingtième* (a form of income tax from which the nobles and officials were usually exempt). There were also indirect taxes that everyone paid: the salt tax, or gabelle, which represented nearly one-tenth of royal revenue; the *traites*, or customs duty, internal and external; and the *aides*, or excise taxes, levied on the sale of items as diverse as wine, tobacco, and iron. All the indirect taxes were extremely unpopular and had much to do with the state's inability to rally the rural masses to its side in 1789. In the 1740s attempts had been made to amend this system but had foundered on the *parlements'*

THE FRENCH REVOLUTION, NAPOLEON, AND THE REPUBLIC:
LIBERTÉ, ÉGALITÉ, AND FRATERNITÉ

The largely irrational tax system in pre-Revolutionary France was another contributing factor to unrest among the lower classes. In this political cartoon, a clergyman and a nobleman stare down at the French farmer, who is crushed by taxes.

opposition to a more equitable distribution of taxation. By 1770 the swelling debt made it obvious that something should be done. Unpopular measures, such as forced loans, were put into effect. Joseph-Marie Terray, Louis XV's comptroller general of finances, repudiated a part of the debt.

Some observers, partisans of enlightened despotism—such as Voltaire, who defended it indirectly in his play of 1773 titled *Les lois de Minos* (The laws of Minos)—argued that the French monarchy stood in this particular instance for administrative rationalization and progress. But the current of opinion was already moving against the crown. Many writers saw in Terray a tool of royal despotism, plain and simple, and his ministerial colleague René-Nicolas-Charles-Augustin de Maupeou (1714–92) was even more detested for his destruction of the *parlements*, which had become the bastion of conservative opposition to royal reform.

PARLEMENTS

The 13 *parlements* (that of Paris being by far the most important) were by their origins law courts. Although their apologists claimed in 1732 that the *parlements* had emerged from the ancient *judicium Francorum* of the Frankish tribes, they had in fact been created by the king in the Middle Ages to dispense justice in his name. With the atrophy of the Estates-General, which had not met since 1614, the *parlements* now claimed to represent the Estates when those were not in session. In 1752 a Jansenist *parlementaire*, Louis-Adrien Le Paige, developed the idea that the various *parlements* should be thought of as the "classes" or parts of a larger and single "Parlement de France."

This was a politically significant claim because these courts had taken on many other quasi-administrative functions that were related to charity, education, the supervision of the police, and even ecclesiastical discipline. Royal decrees were not binding, claimed the *parlementaires*, unless the *parlements* had registered them as laws. Although the *parlementaires* admitted that the king might force them to register his decrees by staging a *lit-de-justice* (i.e., by appearing in person at their session), they also knew that the

THE FRENCH REVOLUTION, NAPOLEON, AND THE REPUBLIC:
LIBERTÉ, ÉGALITÉ, AND FRATERNITÉ

THE TAILLE AND CAPITATION TAXES

The taille was the most important direct tax of the prerevolutionary monarchy in France. Its unequal distribution, with clergy and nobles exempt, made it one of the hated institutions of the ancien régime.

The taille originated in the early Middle Ages as an arbitrary exaction from peasants. Often commuted or renounced after 1150, it was revived in regulated forms in the later Middle Ages. During the Hundred Years' War (1337-1453), the king's seigneurial taille raised from his domain, was extended throughout France to meet expenses, and it developed into the royal taille. Since the taille was a monetary equivalent for military service, the nobility, who fought, and the clergy, who were exempt from fighting did not pay, so that the tax fell on nonprivileged persons and lands. Under Charles VII (ruled 1422-61) the collection of the taille was formally organized and made permanent and exclusively royal. The taille had become an indispensable source of royal revenue and continued to be collected by the French kings until the Revolution at an ever-increasing rate.

By the 18th century the many exemptions to payment of the taille made it weigh more heavily on those who still were liable to pay it. Inhabitants of large towns, such as Paris and Lyon, did not have to pay, and an ever-increasing number of judicial and financial offices carried with them the right of ennoblement, giving the holders the enviable social status of non-taillables.

The other major direct tax in France before the Revolution of 1789 was the capitation. The capitation was first established in 1695 as a wartime measure. Originally, the capitation was to be paid by every subject, the amount varying according to class. For the purpose of the tax, French society was divided into 22 classes, ranging from members of the royal family, who owed 2,000 livres (basic monetary unit of pre-revolutionary France) to day workers who owed only one livre. The tax became permanent in the early 18th century. In practice the capitation was merely an addition to the taille, the long-existing royal tax, falling predominantly on the nonprivileged classes of the French people, who paid the bulk of the taxes.

Both the taille and the capitation were abolished with the Revolution of 1789.

public deplored such maneuvers, which manifestly went against the grain of the monarch's supposed Christian and paternalist solicitude for the well-being of his subjects.

Various social, cultural, and institutional developments had served to turn the *parlements* into strongholds of resistance to reforms that increased the crown's powers. Since the 17th century the monarchy's need for money and the ensuing venality of offices had enabled the *parlementaires* to purchase their positions and to become a small and self-conscious elite, a new "nobility of the robe." In 1604 the creation of the *paulette* tax had enabled the *parlementaires* to make their offices a part of their family patrimony, even if the value of their offices fell somewhat during the course of the 18th century. They had gained status by intermarrying with the older chivalric nobility of the sword. By 1700 the *parlementaires* had become a hereditary and rich landowning elite. (Near Bordeaux, for example, the best vineyards were theirs.) The interregnum of the regency after the death of Louis XIV (1715–23) had given them a chance to recapture some of the ground they had lost during Louis's reign; the value of their offices, however, fell again somewhat in the course of the 18th century. The *parlementaires*' Jansenist

THE FRENCH REVOLUTION, NAPOLEON, AND THE REPUBLIC:
LIBERTÉ, ÉGALITÉ, AND FRATERNITÉ

leanings and their recent espousal of antiabsolutism—expressed in the work of Montesquieu, himself a baron and a *parlementaire*—gave this elite ideological consistency.

In 1764 the Jansenist *parlementaires*, as ideological "progressives," secured the expulsion of the Jesuits from France. Incidents such as the death sentence administered by the Parlement of Paris in 1766 against the 18-year-old chevalier de la Barre, accused of mutilating a crucifix and owning a copy of Voltaire's *Dictionnaire philosophique* (1764; *Philosophical Dictionary*), showed, however, that the courts were not entirely on the side of the Enlightenment. In 1768–69 the Parlement of Brittany, in an antiabsolutist stance, forced the resignation of an appointed royal official, the duc d'Aiguillon, who had boldly tried to limit the power of the local nobility, with whom the *parlement* was now in close alliance.

THE KING AND *PARLEMENTS*

In 1770 the conflict with the *parlements* had reached such a level that Louis XV was finally goaded into a burst of absolutist energy. The Paris Parlements, which had dared to attack Terray's financial reform, were dissolved on January 19, 1771. Maupeou was then authorized to create an altogether different set of *parlements*, with appointed judges shorn of administrative and political power.

In time, opinion might well have accepted Terray's and Maupeou's reforms, despite the outcry raised by the *parlements*' supporters, who argued that the arbitrary uprooting of these centuries-old institutions threatened to turn France into a "ministerial despotism." France might then, like Prussia, have avoided revolution from below through the practice of a revolution from above. But the death of Louis XV in 1774 put an end to the experiment. His 20-year-old successor, Louis XVI (reigned 1774–92), unsure of himself and eager to please, recalled the *parlements* and forced Maupeou into retirement.

In late 1774 Louis XVI appointed Turgot, a former intendant, comptroller general. Perhaps because he thought that the success of his reforms would guarantee their acceptance, perhaps also because he thought it vain to attack the Parlement directly so soon after Maupeou's dismissal, Turgot carried through his measures without first destroying the institutional bases of privileged conservatism. He left the Parlement alone and attempted instead to reduce government expenditures and to alter the methods of tax collecting. In accordance with his physiocratic laissez-faire principles, he freed the grain trade from restraint; suppressed the *corvée*, or forced labour service, exacted from the peasants; and

LOUIS XVI, PAINTING BY JOSEPH SIFFRED DUPLESSIS, C. 1774; IN THE MUSÉE DES BEAUX-ARTS IN CHARTRES, FRANCE.

THE FRENCH REVOLUTION, NAPOLEON, AND THE REPUBLIC:
LIBERTÉ, ÉGALITÉ, AND FRATERNITÉ

abolished the guilds, which had limited both access to artisanal professions and the competition within them. Finally, he suggested that Protestants should be given freedom of conscience. In short, Turgot attempted to rationalize the administrative practices of the French state and to individuate French social and economic life. The solution to the financial crisis, he thought, would come not through the state's appropriation of a larger share of extant resources but from the expansion of the nation's ability to produce and pay. The strength of creative individualism, he thought, would break the political impasse.

In May 1776, however, Turgot was dismissed. Opposition to his measures had come from all sides: a poor harvest had sparked peasant disturbances, the clericalists were antagonized by Turgot's philosophical friends (his greatest and most loyal disciple was Marie-Jean-Antoine-Nicolas de Caritat, marquis de Condorcet, the future Girondin), and, when the Parlement of Paris once again refused to register the new edicts, Louis abandoned Turgot as he had dismissed Maupeou. Thenceforth, the state carried through only minor reforms, none of them on a scale commensurate with the needs felt by the Enlightenment bourgeoisie and notables of the cities and towns. The vestiges of serfdom were suppressed in 1779, and in 1780 torture was abolished. In 1784 the king's use of lettres de cachet for purposes of arbitrary imprisonment without trial was considerably curtailed. But these were minor adjustments. Nothing was done to solve the fundamental problems of the organization of society and of the state in a manner that would be acceptable to progressive public opinion.

The issue of fundamental reform came to the fore again in 1786, when the loans floated to pay for the American war began to come due, and the controller general, Charles-Alexandre de Calonne (1734–1802), had to tell the king that they could not be repaid. "The only way to bring real order into the finances is to revitalize the entire state by reforming all that is defective in its constitution," Calonne told his sovereign.

Although Louis XVI accepted Calonne's proposal to convene an Assembly of Notables, chosen from the country's elites, and to seek their endorsement for a comprehensive reform program, the monarchy had already frittered away the prestige and authority that might have allowed this gamble to succeed. Repeated changes of policy in the previous decades had made the public wary of royal initiatives. Louis XV's sexual adventures, especially his public liaison with Mme du Barry, widely rumoured to have once been a prostitute, had severely damaged the monarchy's image. Louis XVI's embarrassing inability to consummate his marriage with Marie-Antoinette for seven years also undermined respect for the

An oil portrait of Marie-Antoinette, Queen of France, was painted in 1783 by Elisabeth Vigée-Lebrun. It is in the National Gallery of Art in Washington, D.C.

THE FRENCH REVOLUTION, NAPOLEON, AND THE REPUBLIC:
LIBERTÉ, ÉGALITÉ, AND FRATERNITÉ

AFFAIR OF THE DIAMOND NECKLACE

The Affair of the Diamond Necklace was a scandal at the court of Louis XVI in 1785 that discredited the French monarchy on the eve of the French Revolution. It began as an intrigue on the part of an adventuress, the comtesse (countess) de La Motte, to procure, supposedly for Queen Marie-Antoinette but in reality for herself and her associates, a diamond necklace worth 1,600,000 livres. The necklace was the property of the Parisian firm of jewelers Boehmer and Bassenge, who had tried unsuccessfully to sell it, first to Louis XV as a present for his mistress Madame du Barry and later to Louis XVI for the queen.

The countess's scheme involved the prestigious Cardinal de Rohan, bishop of Strasbourg, who as French ambassador to Vienna from 1772 to 1774 had aroused the dislike of the queen's mother, the empress Maria Theresa, and who had subsequently incurred the hostility of Marie-Antoinette herself; he was anxious to be restored to favour at the French court.

The comtesse de La Motte suggested to the cardinal that the queen wished to acquire the necklace surreptitiously and would be prepared for a formal reconciliation at court if he would facilitate its purchase by negotiating with the jewelers. After reading forged letters supposedly from the queen and after a brief nocturnal interview in the gardens of Versailles with a prostitute disguised as the queen, the cardinal entered into a contract with the jewelers to pledge his credit to pay for the necklace in installments. The imposture came to light, however, when the cardinal failed to raise the first installment in full and the jewelers applied directly to the queen. With the imposture exposed, it was discovered that the necklace that the cardinal had supposed to be in the queen's possession had been broken up and sold in London.

> Instead of concealing the intrigue, Louis XVI had the cardinal arrested and imprisoned in the Bastille. The cardinal was tried, along with his alleged accomplices, before the Parlement of Paris. Though he was eventually acquitted of the charge of having fraudulently acquired the necklace (May 31, 1786), he was deprived of all his offices and exiled to the abbey of La Chaise-Dieu in Auvergne. The comtesse de La Motte was sentenced to be flogged, branded, and imprisoned for life in the Salpêtrière prison in Paris. She later escaped to England and there published scandalous *Mémoires* vilifying the queen.
>
> Though Marie-Antoinette was guiltless, the scandal confirmed the belief of contemporaries in her moral laxness and frivolity. The arbitrary arrest of the cardinal, the pressure put on his judges, and his final disgrace deepened the impression of the king's weakness and the autocratic nature of his government. The incident was one of many factors leading to the dissolution of the ancien régime and thus to the French Revolution. The Affair of the Diamond Necklace has been retold in literature and film.

throne, which suffered a further blow from the Affair of the Diamond Necklace of 1785–86, in which a high-ranking prelate was accused of having tried to seduce the queen.

The Assembly of Notables that Calonne had suggested met in February 1787. The minister presented a program that offered the country's upper classes some voice in lawmaking in exchange for their consent to the abolition of many traditional privileges, particularly the nobility's immunity to taxes. Although he did not suggest the creation of a national parliament, Calonne's plan involved the establishment of provincial

THE FRENCH REVOLUTION, NAPOLEON, AND THE REPUBLIC:
LIBERTÉ, ÉGALITÉ, AND FRATERNITÉ

assemblies that would oversee the use of public money. Even though Calonne's proposals were a major step in the direction of representative government and the abolition of special privileges, the notables refused to accept proposals put forward by a minister whom they held responsible for previously worsening the deficit. Desperate to obtain badly needed new revenues, Louis XVI replaced Calonne with Loménie de Brienne, archbishop of Toulouse, who had been one of Calonne's strongest critics in the Assembly of Notables. Almost at once Loménie reversed himself and came to Calonne's conclusion: the state could not go on as it had. The notables, however, refused to be more amenable to Loménie than they had been to Calonne. Despairing of securing the consent of the privileged orders, Loménie dismissed the assembly in May of 1787, and in August the Paris Parlement was exiled to Troyes.

But these measures were desperate, and already the monarchy was beginning to lose control of the political process. Indeed, for the next two years it floundered from one scheme to another in the impossible hope of squaring the circle of modernistic reform, popular hostility, respect of privilege, and the preservation of royal absolutism. Essentially unwilling to force the privileged notables to yield their corporate rights, the crown was unable to assert any coherent policy. The Parlement was therefore recalled from Troyes in September 1787, again dismissed in May 1788, and, in the face of the beginning of a breakdown of law and order and of the inability of officials to collect taxes, once more recalled to Paris by the crown in August 1788.

By this time, the government had already announced the summoning of a national representative assembly, the Estates-General. All the king's subjects would be allowed to participate in choosing representatives and in drafting lists of grievances, called *cahiers de doléances*, in which they could voice their opinions about the problems facing the kingdom. When the just-restored Parlement of Paris, concerned to prevent ministerial manipulation of the Estates-General, rushed to declare that it should be structured "according to the forms of 1614," with the two privileged orders (the clergy and the nobility) having separate chambers and a veto on all legislation, the judges quickly lost most of their popularity. Leadership of the movement for political reform passed to new men who had no stake in preserving old institutions.

Self-proclaimed "patriot" pamphleteers such as the abbé Emmanuel-Joseph Sieyès, whose pamphlet *Qu'est-ce que le tiers état?* (1789; *What Is the Third Estate?*) was one of the most widely read of the thousands of tracts published as the royal censorship system ceased to function, demanded that the upcoming assembly be structured so that the Third Estate of commoners, the vast majority of the population, could prevent the privileged orders from paralyzing its deliberations. In a last and fitful assertion of authority, at the behest of Necker, recalled as minister when Loménie was dismissed in August 1788, the crown decided on December 27 to overrule the Paris Parlement. The Estates, it resolved, would meet separately, but the Third Estate would have as many deputies as the other two orders combined. The stage was set for the coming Revolution.

THE BUILDUP TO REVOLUTION

In an immediate sense, what brought down the ancien régime was its own inability to change or, more simply, to pay its way.

THE FRENCH REVOLUTION, NAPOLEON, AND THE REPUBLIC:
LIBERTÉ, ÉGALITÉ, AND FRATERNITÉ

The deeper causes for its collapse are more difficult to establish. One school of interpretation maintains that French society under the ancien régime was rent by class war. This position implies that the French Revolution revolved around issues of class; it has led to the class analysis of prerevolutionary society as well as to the class analysis of the opposing Revolutionary factions of Girondins and Montagnards and, more generally, to what the historian Alfred Cobban called "the social interpretation of the French Revolution."

In keeping with this interpretation, Marxist historians from the 1930s to the '70s emphasized that the French 18th-century bourgeoisie had assumed a distinct position in French society in that it was in control of commerce, banking, and industry. Revisionist historians in the 1980s, however, responded that the bourgeoisie had no monopoly in these sectors; nobles were also heavily involved in foreign trade, in banking, and in some of the most modern industries, such as coal mining and chemicals.

Most historians today argue that, on balance, it was becoming increasingly difficult to distinguish clearly between the nobility and the bourgeoisie. Like most nobles, wealthy French nonnobles were landlords and even owners of seigneuries, which were bought and sold before 1789 like any other commodity. Although one can speak of a secularized "bourgeois" ethic of thrift and prudence that had come into its own, supporters of this ethic, as of the Enlightenment ethic, were both noble and nonnoble.

There were two areas, however, in which the nobility enjoyed important institutional privileges: the upper ranks of the army and the clergy were, in the main, aristocratic preserves and had become more so in the 1780s. Henri de Boulainvilliers, in his posthumous essays of 1732 on the nobility of France, had even developed a wholly fraudulent but widely praised theory of noble racial superiority. Thus, there were some issues on which all the bourgeoisie might unite against most of the nobility. But such issues, it is now claimed, were relatively unimportant.

Proponents of a social explanation of the Revolution have also emphasized the role of the lower classes. As population increased during the 18th century, peasant landholdings tended to become smaller, and the gap between rich and poor grew. Although the general trend after 1715 had been one of greater overall prosperity, the 20 years before 1789 were a time of economic difficulties. The months leading up to the convening of the Estates-General coincided with the worst subsistence crisis France had suffered in many years; a spring drought was followed by a devastating hailstorm that ruined crops in much of the northern half of the country in July 1788. Distressed peasants were thus eager to take advantage of a situation in which the privileges of their landlords seemed vulnerable to attack. Urban workers, who suffered acutely when bread prices rose, as they had after Turgot's reforms in 1775 and again after the 1788 hailstorm, also had social grievances. Some felt menaced by the development of large-scale manufacturing enterprises; others resented the regulations that, for example, prevented journeymen from setting up their own shops in competition with privileged guild masters. The process of elections to the Estates-General gave both rural and urban populations an unprecedented opportunity to articulate grievances against elite privileges that had been endemic under the ancien régime but that had not been openly voiced.

THE FRENCH REVOLUTION, NAPOLEON, AND THE REPUBLIC:
LIBERTÉ, ÉGALITÉ, AND FRATERNITÉ

OATH OF THE HORATII, *OIL PAINTING BY JACQUES-LOUIS DAVID, 1784; IN THE LOUVRE, PARIS.*

Contemporary historiography has refocused the discussion regarding the causes for the Revolution. Studying the representation of politics, the shape of Revolutionary festivals, and the Revolutionary cults of sacrifice and heroism, scholars have come to place the transformation of culture at the core of their discussion. What really mattered was the desanctifying of the monarchy, the new understanding of the self and the public good, and the belief that thinking individuals might seize the state and fundamentally reshape it. Other historians, by contrast, have emphasized the persistent liabilities that French political culture carried through the Enlightenment, such as the suspicion of dissent and the readiness to rely on force to subvert it.

From either of these two perspectives, it follows that the prospects of the monarchy's survival were dim in 1788. Many government officials, it is true, were finely attuned to public opinion. The vast neorepublican canvases of Jacques-Louis David (1748–1845), such as his *Oath of the Horatii* (1784), glorifying traditional republicanism, were commissioned by the king's dispenser of patronage, the marquis d'Angivillers, a friend of Turgot. Visionary architects, developing a style of Revolutionary Neoclassicism, similarly received royal commissions for new public works. Chrétien Guillaume de Lamoignon de Malesherbes (1721–94), another friend of Turgot and, like him, a minister of the crown, protected the Encyclopédistes. On balance, however, it is hard to see how the monarchy, even if it had resolved its financial problems, which it was very far from doing, could have extended this ecumenism from art to politics and social life. To do so, it would have had to transform its institutions in keeping with new conceptions regarding men's public and private affairs and to commit itself to the rejection of the corporatist ethic in economic life. Thus, the monarchy seemed fated to failure and the stage set for revolution.

CHAPTER 3

THE DESTRUCTION OF THE ANCIEN RÉGIME

After 1789 Louis XVI's incapacity to rule, his irresolution, and his surrender to reactionary influences at court were partially responsible for the failure to establish in France the forms of a limited constitutional monarchy. He allowed himself to be persuaded that royal dignity required him to avoid communication with the deputies assembled at Versailles, and he made no attempt to lay out a program that might have attracted their support. At critical moments, he was distracted by the illness and death of his eldest son, the dauphin (June 4, 1789).

By this time the fundamental weakness of the king's character had become evident. Lethargic in temperament, lacking political insight, and therefore incapable of appreciating

THE DESTRUCTION OF THE ANCIEN RÉGIME

the need to compromise, Louis continued to divert himself by hunting and with his personal hobbies of making locks and doing masonry. His dismissal of Necker in early July 1789 would set off popular demonstrations culminating in the storming of the Bastille, which then forced the king to accept the authority of the newly proclaimed National Assembly. Despite his reluctance, he had to endorse its "destruction" of the feudal regime.

THE CONVERGENCE OF REVOLUTIONS, 1789

The year 1789 would prove to be the decisive climax of the early Revolutionary spirit in France. Louis XVI's ineffective leadership—symbolic of the widespread failures of the ancien régime to meet the demands of the French people—had become overly apparent at that point. As the year progressed, decisive revolutions in different areas of French politics and society would come to give shape to a new France—one that would usher in the replacement of outdated systems of governance, taxation, and social structure.

THE JURIDICAL REVOLUTION

Louis XVI's decision to convene the Estates-General in May 1789 became a turning point in French history. When he invited his subjects to express their opinions and grievances in preparation for this event—unprecedented in living memory—hundreds responded with pamphlets in which the liberal ideology of 1789 gradually began to take shape.

THE FRENCH REVOLUTION, NAPOLEON, AND THE REPUBLIC:
LIBERTÉ, ÉGALITÉ, AND FRATERNITÉ

OPENING OF THE ESTATES-GENERAL, MAY 5, 1789, AN OIL PAINTING BY AUGUSTE COUDER DATED 1839, IS IN THE MUSEUM OF THE HISTORY OF FRANCE IN THE PALACE OF VERSAILLES IN VERSAILLES, FRANCE.

Exactly how the Estates-General should deliberate proved to be the pivotal consciousness-raising issue. Each of the three Estates could vote separately (by order) as they had in the distant past, or they could vote jointly (by head). Because the Third Estate was to have twice as many deputies as the others, only voting by head would assure its preponderant influence. If the estates voted by order, the clergy and nobility would effectively exercise a

THE DESTRUCTION OF THE ANCIEN RÉGIME

veto power over important decisions. Most pamphleteers of 1789 considered themselves "patriots," or reformers, and (though some were nobles themselves) identified the excessive influence of "aristocrats" as a chief obstacle to reform. In his influential tract *Qu'est-ce que le tiers état?* (1789; *What Is the Third Estate?*), the constitutional theorist Emmanuel-Joseph Sieyès asserted that the Third Estate really was the French nation. While commoners did all the truly laborious and productive work of society, he claimed with some exaggeration, the nobility monopolized its lucrative sinecures and honours. As a condition of genuine reform, the Estates-General would have to change that situation.

A seismic shift was occurring in elite public opinion. What began in 1787–88 as a conflict between royal authority and traditional aristocratic groups had become a triangular struggle, with "the people" opposing both absolutism and privilege. A new kind of political discourse was emerging, and within a year it was to produce an entirely new concept of sovereignty with extremely far-reaching implications.

Patriots were driven to increasingly bold positions in part by the resistance and bad faith of royal and aristocratic forces. It is not surprising that some of the Third Estate's most radical deputies came from Brittany, whose nobility was so hostile to change that it finally boycotted the Estates-General altogether.

THE FRENCH REVOLUTION, NAPOLEON, AND THE REPUBLIC:
LIBERTÉ, ÉGALITÉ, AND FRATERNITÉ

Hoping that the king would take the lead of the patriot cause, liberals were disappointed at the irresolute, business-as-usual attitude of the monarchy when the Estates opened at Versailles in May 1789. While the nobility organized itself into a separate chamber (by a vote of 141 to 47), as did the clergy (133 to 114), the Third Estate refused to do so. After pleading repeatedly for compromise and debating their course of action in the face of this deadlock, the Third Estate's deputies finally acted decisively. On June 17 they proclaimed that they were not simply the Third Estate of the Estates-General but a National Assembly (Assemblée Nationale), which the other deputies were invited to join. A week later 150 deputies of the clergy did indeed join the National Assembly, but the nobility protested that the whole notion was illegal.

Now the king had to clarify his position. He began by closing the hall assigned to the Third Estate and ordering all deputies to hear a royal address on June 23. The deputies, however, adjourned to an indoor tennis court on the 20th and there swore a solemn oath to continue meeting until they had provided France with a constitution. Two days later they listened to the king's program for reform. In the "royal session" of June 23, the king pledged to honour civil liberties, agreed to fiscal equality (already conceded by the nobility in its cahiers, or grievance petitions), and promised that the Estates-General would meet regularly in the future. But, he declared, they would deliberate separately by order. France was to become a constitutional monarchy, but one in which "the ancient distinction of the three orders will be conserved in its entirety." In effect the king was forging an alliance with the nobility, whose most articulate members—the judges of the *parlements*—only a year before had sought to hobble him. For the patriots this was too little and too late.

THE DESTRUCTION OF THE ANCIEN RÉGIME

In a scene of high drama, the deputies refused to adjourn to their own hall. When ordered to do so by the king's chamberlain, the assembly's president, astronomer Jean-Sylvain Bailly (1736–93), responded—to the official's amazement—that "the assembled nation cannot receive orders." Such defiance unnerved the king. Backing down, he directed the nobles several days later to join a National Assembly whose existence he had just denied. Thus, the Third Estate, with its allies in the clergy and nobility, had apparently effected a successful nonviolent revolution from above. Having been elected in the *bailliages* (the monarchy's judicial districts, which served as electoral circumscriptions) to represent particular constituents to their king, the deputies had transformed themselves into representatives of the entire nation. Deeming the nation alone to be sovereign, they, as its representatives, claimed sole authority to exercise that sovereignty. This was the juridical revolution of 1789.

PARISIAN REVOLT

In fact, the king had by no means reconciled himself to this revolutionary act. His concession was a strategic retreat until he could muster the military power to subdue the patriots. Between June 27 and July 1 he ordered 20,000 royal troops into the Paris region, ostensibly to protect the assembly and to prevent disorder in the restive capital. The assembly's pleas to the king to withdraw these menacing and unnecessary troops fell on deaf ears. For all of their moral force, the deputies utterly lacked material force to counter the king's obvious intentions. The assembly was saved from likely dissolution only by a massive popular mobilization.

THE FRENCH REVOLUTION, NAPOLEON, AND THE REPUBLIC:
LIBERTÉ, ÉGALITÉ, AND FRATERNITÉ

During the momentous political events of 1788–89, much of the country lay in the grip of a classic subsistence crisis. Bad weather had reduced the grain crops that year by almost one-quarter the normal yield. An unusually cold winter compounded the problem, as frozen rivers halted the transport and milling of flour in many localities. Amid fears of hoarding and profiteering, grain and flour reserves dwindled. In Paris the price of the four-pound loaf of bread—the standard item of consumption accounting for most of the population's calories and nutrition—rose from its usual 8 sous to 14 sous by January 1789. This intolerable trend set off traditional forms of popular protest. If royal officials did not assure basic food supplies at affordable prices, then people would act directly to seize food. During the winter and spring of 1789, urban consumers and peasants rioted at bakeries and markets and attacked millers and grain convoys. Then, in July, this anxiety merged with the looming political crisis at Versailles. Parisians believed that food shortages and royal troops would be used in tandem to starve the people and overwhelm them into submission. They feared an "aristocratic plot" to throttle the patriot cause.

When the king dismissed the still-popular finance minister Necker on July 11, Parisians correctly read this as a signal that the counterrevolution was about to begin. Instead of yielding, however, they rose in rebellion. Street-corner orators such as Camille Desmoulins stirred their compatriots to resist. Confronting royal troops in the streets, they won some soldiers to their side and induced officers to confine other potentially unreliable units to their barracks. On July 13, bands of Parisians ransacked armourers' shops in a frantic search for weapons. The next day a large crowd invaded the Hôtel des Invalides and seized thousands of rifles without resistance. Then they moved to the Bastille, an

THE DESTRUCTION OF THE ANCIEN RÉGIME

An illustration shows people attacking the prison known as the Bastille on July 14, 1789. This event is considered the beginning of the French Revolution and is celebrated every year in France on Bastille Day.

old fortress commanding the Faubourg Saint-Antoine, which had served as a notorious royal prison earlier in the century but was now scheduled for demolition. Believing that gunpowder was stored there, the crowd laid siege to the Bastille. Unlike the troops at the Invalides, the Bastille's tiny garrison resisted, a fierce battle erupted, and dozens of Parisians were killed. When the garrison finally capitulated, the irate crowd massacred several of the soldiers. In another part of town two leading royal officials were lynched for their presumed role in the plot against the

THE FRENCH REVOLUTION, NAPOLEON, AND THE REPUBLIC:
LIBERTÉ, ÉGALITÉ, AND FRATERNITÉ

THE FLAG OF FRANCE

Under the ancien régime, France had a great number of flags, and many of its military and naval flags were elaborate and subject to artistic variations. The royal coat of arms, a blue shield with three golden fleurs-de-lis, was the basis for the state flag. After the Bourbons came to power, this shield was generally displayed against a background of the Bourbon dynastic colour, white.

The French Revolution of 1789 led to an emphasis on simple flag designs that expressed the radical changes being introduced into social, political, and economic life. Blue and red, the traditional colours of Paris, were popular among revolutionaries in that city, and the Bourbon royal white was often added. In 1790 three equal vertical stripes, arranged red-white-blue within a frame of the same colours, were added to the white flag of the navy. Four years later the Tricolour, with stripes now ordered blue-white-red, was made the official national flag for use by the common people, the army, and the navy. This flag was seen to embody all the principles of the revolution—liberty, equality, fraternity, democracy, secularism, and modernization. Many other nations, especially in Europe, adopted tricoloured flags in imitation of the French, replacing its colours with their own. In this way the French Tricolour has become one of the most influential national flags in history, standing in symbolic opposition to the autocratic and clericalist royal standards of the past as well as to the totalitarian banners of modern communism and fascism.

With two brief interruptions (during the Bourbon Restoration in 1814/15 and for two weeks in 1848), the Tricolour has been the sole national flag of France and of all territories under its control.

people. Meanwhile, the electors of Paris, who had continued to meet after choosing their deputies to the Estates-General, ousted the royal officials of the city government, formed a revolutionary municipality, and organized a citizens' militia, or national guard, to patrol the streets. Similar municipal revolutions occurred in 26 of the 30 largest French cities, thus assuring that the capital's defiance would not be an isolated act.

By any standard, the fall of the Bastille to the Parisian crowd was a spectacular symbolic event—a seemingly miraculous triumph of the people against the power of royal arms. The heroism of the crowd and the blood of its martyrs—ordinary Parisian artisans, tradesmen, and workers—sanctified the patriot cause. Most important, the elites and the people of Paris had made common cause, despite the inherent distrust and social distance between them. The mythic unity of the Third Estate—endlessly invoked by patriot writers and orators—seemed actually to exist, if only momentarily. Before this awesome material and moral force, Louis XVI capitulated. He did not want civil war in the streets. The Parisian insurrection of July 14 not only saved the National Assembly from dissolution but altered the course of the Revolution by giving it a far more active, popular, and violent dimension. On July 17 the king traveled to Paris, where he publicly donned a cockade bearing a new combination of colours: white for the Bourbons and blue and red for the city of Paris. This tricolour was to become the new national flag.

PEASANT INSURGENCIES

Peasants in the countryside, meanwhile, carried on their own kind of rebellion, which combined traditional aspirations and

THE FRENCH REVOLUTION, NAPOLEON, AND THE REPUBLIC:
LIBERTÉ, ÉGALITÉ, AND FRATERNITÉ

anxieties with support of the patriot cause. The peasant revolt was autonomous, yet it reinforced the urban uprising to the benefit of the National Assembly.

Competition over the ownership and use of land had intensified in many regions. Peasants owned only about 40 percent of the land, leasing or sharecropping the rest from the nobility, the urban middle class, and the church. Population growth and subdivision of the land from generation to generation was reducing the margin of subsistence for many families. Innovations in estate management—the grouping of leaseholds, conversion of arable land to pasture, enclosure of open fields, division of common land at the lord's initiative, discovery of new seigneurial dues or arrears in old ones—exasperated peasant tenants and smallholders. Historians debate whether these were capitalistic innovations or traditional varieties of seigneurial extraction, but in either case the countryside was boiling with discontent over these trends as well as over oppressive royal taxes and food shortages. Peasants were poised between great hopes for the future raised by the calling of the Estates-General and extreme anxiety—fear of losing land, fear of hunger (especially after the catastrophic harvest of 1788), and fear of a vengeful aristocracy.

In July peasants in several regions sacked the castles of nobles and burned the documents that recorded their feudal obligations. This peasant insurgency eventually merged into the movement known as the Great Fear. Rumours abounded that these vagrants were actually brigands in the pay of nobles, who were marching on villages to destroy the new harvest and coerce the peasants into submission. The fear was baseless, but hundreds of false alarms and panics stirred up hatred and suspicion of nobles, led peasants to arm themselves as best they could, and set off widespread attacks on châteaus and feudal

THE DESTRUCTION OF THE ANCIEN RÉGIME

documents. The peasant revolt suggested that the unity of the Third Estate against "aristocrats" extended from Paris to villages across the country. The Third Estate truly seemed invincible.

THE ABOLITION OF FEUDALISM

Of course the violence of peasant insurgency worried the deputies of the National Assembly; to some it seemed as if the countryside were being engulfed by anarchy that threatened all property. But the majority were unwilling to turn against the rebellious peasants. Instead of denouncing the violence, they tried to appease peasant opinion. Liberal nobles and clergy began the session of August 4 by renouncing their ancient feudal privileges. Within hours the assembly was propelled into decreeing "the abolition of feudalism" as well as the church tithe, venality of office, regional privilege, and fiscal privilege. A few days later, to be sure, the assembly clarified the August 4 decree to assure that "legitimate" seigneurial property rights were maintained. While personal feudal servitudes such as hunting rights, seigneurial justice, and labour services were suppressed outright, most seigneurial dues were to be abolished only if the peasants paid compensation to their lords, set at 20 to 25 times the annual value of the obligation. The vast majority of peasants rejected that requirement by passive resistance, until pressure built in 1792–93 for the complete abolition of all seigneurial dues without compensation.

The abolition of feudalism was crucial to the evolution of a modern, contractual notion of property and to the development of an unimpeded market in land. But it did not directly affect the ownership of land or the level of ordinary rents and leases. Seigneurs lost certain kinds of traditional income, but

THE FRENCH REVOLUTION, NAPOLEON, AND THE REPUBLIC:
LIBERTÉ, ÉGALITÉ, AND FRATERNITÉ

they remained landowners and landlords. While all peasants gained in dignity and status, only the landowning peasants came out substantially ahead economically. Tenant farmers found that what they had once paid for the tithe was added on to their rent. And the assembly did virtually nothing to assure better lease terms for renters and sharecroppers, let alone their acquisition of the land they tilled.

THE NEW REGIME

By sweeping away the old web of privileges, the August 4 decree permitted the assembly to construct a new regime. Since it would take months to draft a constitution, the assembly on August 27 promulgated its basic principles in a Declaration of the Rights of Man and of the Citizen. A rallying point for the future, the declaration also stood as the death certificate of the ancien régime. The declaration's authors believed it to have universal significance. "In the new hemisphere, the brave inhabitants of Philadelphia have given the example of a people who reestablished their liberty," conceded one deputy, but "France would give that example to the rest of the world." At the same time, the declaration responded to particular circumstances and was thus a calculated mixture of general principles and specific concerns. Its concept of natural rights meant that the Revolution would not be bound by history and tradition but could reshape the contours of society according to reason—a position vehemently denounced by Edmund Burke in England.

The very first article of the declaration resoundingly challenged Europe's old order by affirming that "men are born and remain free and equal in rights. Social distinctions may be based

THE DESTRUCTION OF THE ANCIEN RÉGIME

only on common utility." Most of its articles concerned individual liberty, but the declaration's emphasis fell equally on the prerogatives of the state as expressed through law. (Considering how drastically the erstwhile delegates to the Estates-General had exceeded their mandates, they certainly needed to underscore the legitimacy of their new government and its laws.) The declaration, and subsequent Revolutionary constitutions, channeled the sovereignty of the nation into representative government, thereby negating claims by *parlements*, provincial estates, or divine-right monarchs as well as any conception of direct democracy. Though the declaration affirmed the separation of powers, by making no provision for a supreme court, it effectively left the French legislature as the ultimate judge of its own actions. The declaration defined liberty as "the ability to do whatever does not harm another…whose limits can only be determined by law." The same limitation by positive law was attached to specific liberties, such as freedom from arbitrary arrest, freedom of expression, and freedom of religious conscience. The men of 1789 believed deeply in these liberties, yet they did not establish them in autonomous, absolute terms that would ensure their sanctity under any circumstances.

RESTRUCTURING FRANCE

From 1789 to 1791 the National Assembly acted as a constituent assembly, drafting a constitution for the new regime while also governing from day to day. The constitution established a limited monarchy, with a clear separation of powers in which the king was to name and dismiss his ministers. But sovereignty effectively resided in the legislative branch, to consist of a single

THE FRENCH REVOLUTION, NAPOLEON, AND THE REPUBLIC:
LIBERTÉ, ÉGALITÉ, AND FRATERNITÉ

house, the Legislative Assembly, elected by a system of indirect voting. ("The people or the nation can have only one voice, that of the national legislature," wrote Sieyès. "The people can speak and act only through its representatives.") Besides failing to win a bicameral system, the moderate Anglophile, or *monarchien*, faction lost a bitter debate on the king's veto power: the assembly granted the king only a suspensive or delaying veto over legislation; if a bill passed the Legislative Assembly in three successive sessions, it would become law even without royal approval.

Dismayed at what he deemed the ill-considered radicalism of such decisions, Jean-Joseph Mounier, a leading patriot deputy in the summer of 1789 and author of the Tennis Court Oath, resigned from the assembly in October. In a similar vein, some late-20th-century historians (notably François Furet) suggested that the assembly's integral concept of national sovereignty and legislative supremacy effectively reestablished absolutism in a new guise, providing the new government with inherently unlimited powers. Nor, they believed, is it surprising that the revolutionaries abused those powers as their pursuit of utopian goals encountered resistance. In theory this may well be true, but it must be balanced against the actual institutions created to implement those powers and the spirit in which they were used. With a few exceptions—notably the religious issue—the National Assembly acted in a liberal spirit, more pragmatic than utopian, and was decidedly more constructive than repressive.

The revolutionaries took civil equality seriously but created a limited definition of political rights. They effectively transferred political power from the monarchy and the privileged estates to the general body of propertied citizens. Nobles

THE DESTRUCTION OF THE ANCIEN RÉGIME

lost their privileges in 1789 and their titles in 1790, but, as propertied individuals, they could readily join the new political elite. The constitution restricted the franchise to "active" citizens who paid a minimal sum in taxes, with higher property qualifications for eligibility for public office (a direct-tax payment equivalent to 3 days' wages for voters and 10 days' wages for electors and officeholders). Under this system about two-thirds of adult males had the right to vote for electors and to choose certain local officials directly. Although it favoured wealthier citizens, the system was vastly more democratic than Britain's.

Predictably, the franchise did not extend to women, despite delegations and pamphlets advocating women's rights. The assembly responded brusquely that, because women were too emotional and easily misled, they must be kept out of public life and devote themselves to their nurturing and maternal roles. But the formal exclusion of women from politics did not keep them on the sidelines. Women were active combatants in local conflicts that soon erupted over religious policy, and they agitated over subsistence issues—Parisian women, for example, made a mass march to Versailles in October that forced the king to move back to the capital. In the towns, they formed auxiliaries to local Jacobin clubs and even a handful of independent women's clubs, participated in civic festivals, and did public relief work.

The assembly's design for local government and administration proved to be one of the Revolution's most durable legacies. Obliterating the political identity of France's historic provinces, the deputies redivided the nation's territory into 83 *départements* of roughly equal size. Unlike the old provinces, each *département* would have exactly the same institutions; *départements* were

THE FRENCH REVOLUTION, NAPOLEON, AND THE REPUBLIC:
LIBERTÉ, ÉGALITÉ, AND FRATERNITÉ

Parisian women returning from Versailles in October 1789, colour lithograph (1789).

in turn subdivided into districts, cantons, and communes (the common designation for a village or town). On the one hand, this administrative transformation promoted decentralization and local autonomy: citizens of each *département*, district, and commune elected their own local officials. On the other hand, these local governments were subordinated to the national legislature and ministries in Paris. The *départements* therefore became instruments of national uniformity and integration, which is to say, centralization. This ambiguity the legislators fully appreciated, assuming that a healthy equilibrium could be maintained

THE DESTRUCTION OF THE ANCIEN RÉGIME

between the two tendencies. That the Revolutionary government of 1793 and Napoleon would later use these structures to concentrate power from the centre was not something they could anticipate.

The new administrative map also created the parameters for judicial reform. Sweeping away the entire judicial system of the ancien régime, the revolutionaries established a civil court in each district and a criminal court in each *département*. At the grass roots they replaced seigneurial justice with a justice of the peace in each canton. Judges on all of these tribunals were to be elected. While rejecting the use of juries in civil cases, the assembly decreed that felonies would be tried by juries; if a jury convicted, judges would merely apply the mandatory sentences set out in the assembly's tough new penal code of 1791. Criminal defendants also gained the right to counsel, which had been denied them under the jurisprudence of the ancien régime. In civil law, the assembly encouraged arbitration and mediation to avoid the time-consuming and costly processes of formal litigation. In general, the revolutionaries hoped to make the administration of justice more accessible and expeditious.

Guided by laissez-faire doctrine and its hostility to privileged corporations, the assembly sought to open up economic life to unimpeded individual initiative and competition. Besides proclaiming the right of all citizens to enter any trade and conduct it as they saw fit, the assembly dismantled internal tariffs and chartered trading monopolies and abolished the guilds of merchants and artisans. Insisting that workers must bargain in the economic marketplace as individuals, the Le Chapelier Law of June 1791 (named after reformer Jean Le Chapelier) banned workers' associations and strikes. The precepts of economic individualism extended to rural life as well. In theory,

THE FRENCH REVOLUTION, NAPOLEON, AND THE REPUBLIC:
LIBERTÉ, ÉGALITÉ, AND FRATERNITÉ

Gouvernements before 1789.

THE DESTRUCTION OF THE ANCIEN RÉGIME

Revolutionary départements after 1789.

THE FRENCH REVOLUTION, NAPOLEON, AND THE REPUBLIC:
LIBERTÉ, ÉGALITÉ, AND FRATERNITÉ

peasants and landlords were now free to cultivate their fields as they wished, regardless of traditional collective routines and constraints. In practice, however, communal restraints proved to be deep-rooted and resistant to legal abolition.

SALE OF NATIONAL LANDS

The Assembly had not lost sight of the financial crisis that precipitated the collapse of absolutism in the first place. Creating an entirely new option for its solution, the Assembly voted to place church property—about 10 percent of the land in France—"at the disposition of the nation." This property was designated as *biens nationaux*, or national lands. The government then issued large-denomination notes called assignats, underwritten and guaranteed by the value of that land. It intended to sell national lands to the public, which would pay for it in assignats that would then be retired. Thus, church property would in effect pay off the national debt and obviate the need for further loans. Unfortunately, the temptation to print additional assignats proved too great. Within a year the assignat evolved into a paper currency in small and large denominations, with sharp inflationary effects.

As the national lands went on sale, fiscal needs took priority over social policy. Sales were arranged in large lots and at auction in the district capitals—procedures that favoured wealthier buyers. True, for about a year in 1793–94, after émigré property was added to the *biens nationaux*, large lots were divided into small parcels. In addition, small-scale peasants acquired some of this land through resale by the original buyers. But overall the urban middle classes and large-scale peasants emerged with the bulk of this land, to the

THE DESTRUCTION OF THE ANCIEN RÉGIME

Assignat of 15 sols, 1790s.

intense frustration of small-scale peasants. The French historian Georges Lefebvre's study of the Nord *département*, for example, found that 7,500 bourgeois purchased 48 percent of the land, while 20,300 peasants bought 52 percent. But the top 10 percent of these peasant purchasers accounted for 60 percent of the peasants' total. Whatever the social origins of the buyers, however, they were likely to be reliable supporters of the Revolution if only to guarantee the security of their new acquisitions.

THE FRENCH REVOLUTION, NAPOLEON, AND THE REPUBLIC:
LIBERTÉ, ÉGALITÉ, AND FRATERNITÉ

SEEDS OF DISCORD

Security could not be taken for granted, however, because the Revolution progressively alienated or disappointed important elements of French society. Among the elites, opposition began almost immediately when some of the king's close relatives left the country in disgust after July 14, thus becoming the first émigrés. Each turning point in the Revolution touched off new waves of emigration, especially among the nobility. By 1792 an estimated two-thirds of the royal officer corps had resigned their commissions, and most had left the country. A contentious royalist press bitterly denounced the policies of the assembly as spoliation and the Revolutionary atmosphere as a form of anarchy. Abroad, widespread enthusiasm for the events in France among the general public from London to Vienna was matched by intense hostility in ruling circles fearful of revolutionary contagion within their own borders.

After the first months of solidarity, long-standing urban-rural tensions took on new force. Though peasants might vote in large numbers, the urban middle classes predictably emerged with the lion's share of the new district and *département* offices after the first elections of 1790. Administrative and judicial reform gave these local officials more powers for intrusion into rural society than royal officials ever had, with battalions of armed national guards to back them up. Peasants might easily view urban revolutionary elites as battening on political power and national lands. And, while the assembly made the tax system more uniform and equitable, direct taxes remained heavy and actually rose in formerly privileged regions, while nothing was done to relieve the plight of tenant farmers. Later, when the Revolutionary government sought to draft young men into the army, another grievance was added to the list.

THE DESTRUCTION OF THE ANCIEN RÉGIME

RELIGIOUS TENSIONS

It was religious policy that most divided French society and generated opposition to the Revolution. Most priests had initially hoped that sweeping reform might return Roman Catholicism to its basic ideals, shorn of aristocratic trappings and superfluous privileges, but they assumed that the church itself would collaborate in the process. In the assembly's view, however, nationalization of church property gave the state responsibility for regulating the church's temporal affairs, such as salaries, jurisdictional boundaries, and modes of clerical appointment. On its own authority the assembly reduced the number of dioceses and realigned their boundaries to coincide with the new *départements*, while requesting local authorities to redraw parish boundaries in conformity with population patterns. Under the Assembly's Civil Constitution of the Clergy (July 1790), bishops were to be elected by *départements*' electoral assemblies, while parish priests were to be chosen by electors in the districts. Clerical spokesmen deplored the notion of lay authority in such matters and insisted that the assembly must negotiate reforms with a national church council.

In November 1790 the assembly forced the issue by requiring all sitting bishops and priests to take an oath of submission. Those who refused would lose their posts, be pensioned off, and be replaced by the prescribed procedures. Throughout France a mere seven bishops complied, while only 54 percent of the parish clergy took the oath. Contrary to the assembly's hopes, the clergy had split in two, with "constitutional" priests on one side and "refractory" priests on the other. Regional patterns accentuated this division: in the west of France, where clerical density was unusually high, only 15 percent of the clergy complied.

THE FRENCH REVOLUTION, NAPOLEON, AND THE REPUBLIC:
LIBERTÉ, ÉGALITÉ, AND FRATERNITÉ

The schism quickly engulfed the laity. As refractories and constitutionals vied for popular support against their rivals, parishioners could not remain neutral. Intense local discord erupted over the implementation of the Civil Constitution of the Clergy. District administrations backed by urban national guards intervened to install "outsiders" chosen to replace familiar or even beloved refractory priests in many parishes; villagers responded by badgering or boycotting the hapless priests who took the oath. Opinion on both sides tended to fateful extremes, linking either the Revolution with impiety or the Roman Catholic Church with counterrevolution.

POLITICAL TENSIONS

The political life of the new regime was also proving more contentious than the revolutionaries had anticipated. With courage and consistency, the assembly had provided that officials of all kinds be elected. But it was uncertain whether these officials, once the ballots were cast, could do their duty free from public pressure and agitation. Nor was it clear what the role of "public opinion" and the mechanisms for its expression would be. The spectacular development of a free press and political clubs provided an answer. Fearful that these extraparliamentary institutions could be abused by demagogues, the assembly tried to curb them from time to time but to no avail. Freed entirely from royal censorship, writers and publishers rushed to satisfy the appetite for news and political opinion. The first journalists included deputies reporting to their constituents by means of a newspaper. Paris, which had only 4 quasi-official newspapers at the start of 1789, saw more than 130 new periodicals by the end of the year, most admittedly short-lived, including 20 dailies. As the journalist Jacques-Pierre Brissot put it, newspapers are "the only way of educating a large nation unaccustomed to freedom or to reading, yet looking to free itself from ignorance." Provincial publishers were as quick to found new periodicals in the larger towns. Bordeaux, for example, had only 1 newspaper in 1789, but 16 appeared within the next two years. While some papers remained bland and politically neutral, many had strong political opinions.

Like the National Assembly, revolutionary clubs also began at Versailles, when patriot deputies rallied to a caucus of outspoken Third Estate deputies from Brittany. Thus began the Club Breton—complete with bylaws, minutes, committees, correspondence, and membership requirements—which later reorganized as the Society of the Friends of the Constitution. Soon it was known as the Jacobin Club, after the Dominican convent where the club met when the assembly transferred to Paris in October. Most prominent revolutionaries belonged to the Jacobin Club, from constitutional royalists such as the comte de Mirabeau, the marquis de Lafayette, and the comte de Barnave to radicals such as Brissot, Alexandre Sabès Pétion, and Maximilien Robespierre. By mid-1791, however, moderates became uncomfortable with the Jacobin Club, where Robespierre was emerging as a dominant figure.

The Jacobin Club was pushed from the left by the Club of the Cordeliers, one of the neighbourhood clubs in the capital. The Cordeliers militants rejected the assembly's concept of representation as the exclusive expression of popular sovereignty. They held to a more direct vision of popular sovereignty as relentless vigilance and participation by citizens through

THE FRENCH REVOLUTION, NAPOLEON, AND THE REPUBLIC:
LIBERTÉ, ÉGALITÉ, AND FRATERNITÉ

demonstrations, petitions, deputations, and, if necessary, insurrection. In his newspaper *L'Ami du peuple* (The friend of the people) Jean-Paul Marat injected an extreme rhetoric about alleged conspiracies and the need for violence against counterrevolutionaries that exceeded anything heard in the assembly's political discourse.

Like the press, clubs quickly spread in the provinces. Building, no doubt, on old-regime patterns of sociability—reading clubs, Freemasonry, or confraternities—political clubs became a prime vehicle for participation in the Revolution. More than 300 towns had clubs by the end of 1790 and 900 by mid-1791. Later clubs spread to the villages as well: a study has counted 5,000 localities that had clubs at one time or another between 1790 and 1795. Many clubs affiliated with the Paris Jacobin Club, the "mother club," in an informal nationwide network. Most began with membership limited to the middle class and a sprinkling of liberal nobles, but gradually artisans, shopkeepers, and peasants joined the rolls. Initially the clubs promoted civic education and publicized the assembly's reforms. But some became more activist, seeking to influence political decisions with petitions, to exercise surveillance over constituted authorities, and to denounce those they deemed remiss.

By 1791 the assembly found itself in a cross fire between the machinations of counterrevolutionaries—émigrés, royalist newspapers, refractory clergy—and the denunciations of radicals. Its ability to steer a stable course depended in part on the cooperation of the king. Publicly Louis XVI distanced himself from his émigré relatives, but privately he was in league with them and secretly corresponded with the royal houses of Spain and Austria to enlist their support. On June 21, 1791,

THE DESTRUCTION OF THE ANCIEN RÉGIME

LE CLUB DES JACOBINS (14 Mai 1790)

Illustrated is a May 14, 1790, convention of the Jacobin Club. As with other revolutionary clubs, the Jacobin Club challenged the effectiveness of the National Assembly and demanded greater vigilance and participation by citizens through protests, petitions, and even insurrections.

the royal family attempted to flee its "captivity" in the Tuileries Palace and escape across the Belgian border. Rashly, Louis left behind a letter revealing his utter hostility to the Revolution. At the last minute, however, the king was recognized at the town of Varennes near the border, and the royal party was forcibly returned to Paris.

A great crisis for the Revolution ensued. While the assembly reinforced the frontiers by calling for 100,000

75

THE FRENCH REVOLUTION, NAPOLEON, AND THE REPUBLIC:
LIBERTÉ, ÉGALITÉ, AND FRATERNITÉ

volunteers from the national guard, its moderate leaders hoped that this fiasco would end Louis's opposition once and for all. To preserve their constitutional compromise, they turned a blind eye to the king's manifest treason by inventing the fiction that he had been kidnapped. As Antoine Barnave put it, "Are we or are we not going to terminate the Revolution? Or are we going to start it all over again?" Outside the assembly, however, Jacobins and Cordeliers launched a petition campaign against reinstating the king. A mass demonstration on July 17 at the Champ de Mars against the king ended in a bloody riot, as the authorities called out the national guard under Lafayette's command to disperse the demonstrators. This precipitated vehement recriminations in the Jacobin Club, which finally split apart under the pressure. The mass of moderate deputies abandoned the club to a rump of radicals and formed a new association called the Club of the Feuillants. Under the leadership of Robespierre and Jérôme Pétion (who later became mortal enemies), the purged Jacobin Club rallied most provincial clubs and emerged from the crisis with a more unified, radical point of view. For the time being, however, the moderates prevailed in the assembly. They completed the Constitution of 1791, and on the last day of September 1791 the National Assembly dissolved itself, having previously decreed the ineligibility of its members for the new Legislative Assembly.

When the newly elected Legislative Assembly convened in October, the question of counterrevolution dominated its proceedings. Such Jacobin deputies as Brissot argued that only war against the émigré army gathering at Coblenz across the Rhine could end the threat: "Do you wish at one blow to

THE DESTRUCTION OF THE ANCIEN RÉGIME

destroy the aristocracy, the refractory priests, and the malcontents: then destroy Coblenz." Whereas the Feuillants opposed this war fever, Lafayette saw a successful military campaign as a way to gain power, while the king's circle believed that war would bring military defeat to France and a restoration of royal authority. On the other side, the Habsburg monarch, Leopold II, had resisted the pleas of his sister Marie-Antoinette and opposed intervention against France, but his death in March 1792 brought his bellicose son Francis II to the throne, and the stage was set for war.

In April 1792 France went to war against a coalition of Austria, Prussia, and the émigrés. Each camp expected rapid victory, but both were disappointed. The allies repulsed a French offensive and soon invaded French territory. The Legislative Assembly called for a new levy of 100,000 military volunteers, but, when it voted to incarcerate refractory clergy, the king vetoed the decree. Though many Frenchmen remained respectful of the king, the most vocal elements of public opinion denounced Louis and demonstrated against him; but the Legislative Assembly refused to act. As Prussian forces drove toward Paris, their commander, the duke of Brunswick, proclaimed his aim of restoring the full authority of the monarchy and warned that any action against the king would bring down "exemplary and memorable vengeance" against the capital. Far from terrifying the Parisians, the Brunswick Manifesto enraged them and drove them into decisive action.

Militants in the Paris Commune, the Revolutionary government of Paris set up by the capital's 48 wards, or sections, gave the Legislative Assembly a deadline in which to

THE FRENCH REVOLUTION, NAPOLEON, AND THE REPUBLIC:
LIBERTÉ, EGALITÉ, AND FRATERNITÉ

suspend the king. When it passed unheeded, they organized an insurrection. On August 10, 1792, a huge crowd of armed Parisians stormed the royal palace after a fierce battle with the garrison. The Legislative Assembly then had no choice but to declare the king suspended. That night more than half the deputies themselves fled Paris, for the Legislative Assembly, too, had lost its mandate. Those who remained ordered the election by universal male suffrage of a National Convention. It would judge the king, draft a new republican constitution, and govern France during the emergency. The Constitution of 1791 had lasted less than a year, and the second revolution dreaded by the Feuillants had begun.

4

THE FIRST FRENCH REPUBLIC

After the overthrow of the monarchy on August 10, 1792, an assembly by the name of the National Convention was elected to provide a new constitution for the country. It would govern France from September 20, 1792, until October 26, 1795, during the most critical period of the French Revolution. The convention numbered 749 deputies, including businessmen, tradesmen, and many professional men. Among its early acts were the formal abolition of the monarchy (September 21) and the establishment of the First French Republic (September 22).

THE SECOND REVOLUTION

The insurrection of August 10, 1792, did not, of course, stop the Prussian advance on the capital. As enthusiastic contingents of

THE FRENCH REVOLUTION, NAPOLEON, AND THE REPUBLIC:
LIBERTÉ, EGALITÉ, AND FRATERNITÉ

volunteers left for the front, fear of counterrevolutionary plots gripped the capital. Journalists such as Jean-Paul Marat pointed to the prisons bursting with vagrants and criminals as well as refractory clergy and royalists and asked what would happen if traitors forced open the jails and released these hordes of fanatics and brigands. In response, Parisians took the law into their own hands with an orgy of mass lynching.

On their own initiative, citizens entered the prisons, set up "popular tribunals" to hold perfunctory trials, and summarily executed between 1,100 and 1,400 prisoners out of a total of 2,800, stabbing and hacking them to death with any instruments at hand. These prison massacres were no momentary fit of frenzy but went on for four days. At the time, no one in authority dared try to stop the slaughter. Officials of the provisional government and the Paris Commune "drew a veil" over this appalling event as it ran its course, though soon political rivals were accusing each other of instigating the massacres. In a different vein, Robespierre among others concluded that popular demands for vengeance and terror had to be channeled into legal forms; to prevent such anarchy, the state itself must become the orderly instrument of the people's punitive will.

The next two weeks brought this period of extreme uncertainty to a close. On September 20 the French army turned back the invaders at the Battle of Valmy, and in November at the Battle of Jemappes it won control of the Austrian Netherlands (now Belgium). On September 21 the National Convention convened, ending the vacuum of authority that had followed the August 10 insurrection. Its first major task was to decide the fate of the ex-king. The convention's trial of Louis became an educational experience for the French people in which the institution of monarchy was to be completely desacralized.

THE FIRST FRENCH REPUBLIC

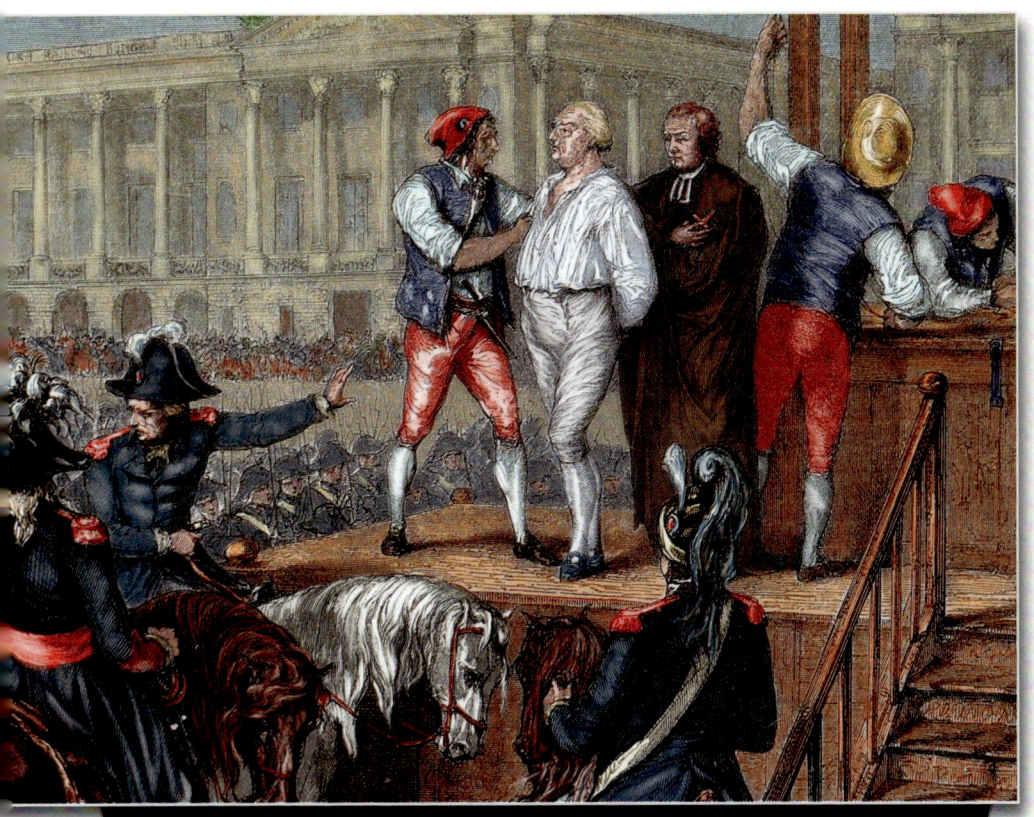

THE EXECUTION OF LOUIS XVI IN 1793.

Hard evidence of Louis's treason produced a unanimous guilty verdict, but the issue of punishment divided the deputies sharply. In a painstaking and solemn debate each deputy cast his vote individually and explained it. At the end the convention voted the death sentence, 387 to 334. A motion for reprieve was defeated (380 to 310), and one to submit the verdict to a national referendum was rejected (425 to 286). This ill-considered proposal left the impression that certain deputies were frantic to save the king's life, and their Jacobin opponents were quick to raise vague accusations of treasonous intent against them. In

THE FRENCH REVOLUTION, NAPOLEON, AND THE REPUBLIC:
LIBERTÉ, ÉGALITÉ, AND FRATERNITÉ

any event, the former king Louis XVI, now known simply as Citizen Capet, was executed on January 21, 1793, in an act of immense symbolic importance. For the deputies to the National Convention, now regicides, there could be no turning back. Laws to deport the refractory clergy, to bar the émigrés forever upon pain of death, and to confiscate their property rounded out the convention's program for eliminating the Revolution's most determined enemies.

A REPUBLIC IN CRISIS

By the spring of 1793, however, the republic was beleaguered. In the second round of the war, the coalition—now reinforced by Spain, Piedmont, and Britain—routed French forces in the Austrian Netherlands and the Rhineland and breached the Pyrenees. Fighting on five different fronts and bereft of effective leadership, French armies seemed to be losing everywhere. Even General Charles-François du Périer Dumouriez, the hero of the first Netherlands campaign, had gone over to the enemy in April after quarreling with the convention. Meanwhile, civil war had broken out within France. Rural disaffection in western France, especially over the religious question referred to earlier, had been building steadily, leaving republicans in the region's cities and small towns an unpopular and vulnerable minority. Rural rage finally erupted into armed rebellion in March 1793 when the convention decreed that each *département* must produce a quota of citizens for the army. In four *départements* south of the Loire River, the Vendée rebellion began with assaults on the towns and the massacre of patriots. Gradually, royalist nobles assumed the leadership of the peasants and weavers who had risen on their own initiative. Forging them into a "Catholic and Royalist Army," they hoped to overthrow the republic and restore the Bourbons.

The convention could take no comfort from the economic situation either. An accelerating depreciation of the assignats compounded severe shortages of grain and flour in 1793. Inflation, scarcity, and hoarding made life unbearable for the urban masses and hampered efforts to provision the republic's armies. In reaction to such economic hardships and to the advance of antirepublican forces at the frontiers and within France, Parisian radicals clamoured relentlessly for decisive action such as price controls and the repression of counterrevolutionaries.

GIRONDINS AND MONTAGNARDS

The Convention was bitterly divided almost to the point of paralysis. From the opening day, two outspoken groups of deputies vied for the support of their less factional colleagues. The roots of this rivalry lay in a conflict between Robespierre and Brissot for leadership of the Jacobin Club in the spring and summer of 1792. At that time Robespierre had argued almost alone against the war that Brissot passionately advocated. Later, when the war went badly and the Brissotins, anxious to wield executive power, acted equivocally in their relations with the king, the Jacobins turned on them. Brissot was formally expelled from the club in October, but his expulsion merely formalized a division that had already crystallized during the elections to the convention in the previous month.

THE FRENCH REVOLUTION, NAPOLEON, AND THE REPUBLIC:
LIBERTÉ, ÉGALITÉ, AND FRATERNITÉ

The Paris electoral assembly sent Robespierre, Marat, Georges Danton, and other stalwarts of the Paris Commune and the Jacobin Club to the convention, while systematically rejecting Brissot and his allies such as the former mayor of Paris, Pétion. The Parisian deputies and their provincial supporters, numbering between 200 and 300 (depending on which historian's taxonomy one accepts), took seats on the convention's upper benches and came to be known as the Montagnards.

Supported by a network of journalists and by politicians such as Interior Minister Jean-Marie Roland, however, the Brissotins retained their popularity in the provinces and were returned as deputies by other *départements*. In the convention the Brissotin group included most deputies from the *département* of the Gironde, and the group came to be known by their opponents as the Girondins. The inner core of this loose faction, who often socialized in Roland's salon, numbered about 60 or, with their supporters, perhaps 150 to 175.

At bottom the Girondin-Montagnard conflict stemmed from a clash of personalities and ambitions. Over the years, historians have made the case for each side by arguing that their opponents constituted the truly aggressive or obstructive minority seeking to dominate the Convention. Clearly most deputies were put off by the bitter personal attacks that regularly intruded on their deliberations. The two factions differed most over the role of Paris and the best way to deal with popular demands. Though of a middle-class background similar to that of their rivals, the Montagnards sympathized more readily with the sansculottes (the local activists) of the capital and proved temperamentally bolder in their response to economic, military, and political problems. United by an extreme hostility to Parisian militance, the Girondins never forgave the Paris

Commune for its inquisitorial activity after August 10. Indeed, some Girondins did not feel physically secure in the capital. They also appeared more committed to political and economic liberties and therefore less willing to adopt extreme revolutionary measures no matter how dire the circumstances. Ready to set aside similar constitutional scruples, the Montagnards tailored their policies to the imperatives of "revolutionary necessity" and unity.

While the Girondins repeatedly attacked Parisian militants—at one point demanding the dissolution of the Paris Commune and the arrest of its leaders—the Montagnards gradually forged an informal alliance with the sansculottes. Similarly, the Montagnards supported deputies sent "on mission" to the *départements* when they clashed with locally elected officials, while the Girondins tended to back the officials. The Montagnards therefore alienated many moderate republicans in the provinces. As deputies of the centre, or "Plain," such as Bertrand Barère, vainly tried to mediate between the two sides, the convention navigated through this factionalism as best it could and improvised new responses to the crisis: a Revolutionary Tribunal to try political crimes; local surveillance committees to seek out subversives; and a Committee of Public Safety to coordinate measures of revolutionary defense. By the end of May 1793 a majority seemed ready to support the Montagnards.

Believing that the Girondins had betrayed and endangered the republic, the Paris sections (with the connivance of the Montagnards and the Paris Jacobin Club) demanded in petitions that the Convention expel the "perfidious deputies." On May 31 they mounted a mass demonstration, and on June 2 they forced a showdown by deploying armed national

THE FRENCH REVOLUTION, NAPOLEON, AND THE REPUBLIC:
LIBERTÉ, ÉGALITÉ, AND FRATERNITÉ

The imprisonment of the Girondins following their expulsion from the National Convention, undated engraving.

guards around the convention's hall. Backed by a huge crowd of unarmed men and women, their solid phalanx of fixed bayonets made it impossible for the deputies to leave without risking serious violence. Inside, the Montagnards applauded this insurrection as an expression of popular sovereignty, akin to that of July 14 or August 10. When the people thus spoke directly, they argued, the deputies had no choice but to comply. Centrists did everything they could to avoid a purge but in the end decided that only this fateful act could preserve the Revolution's unity. Barère composed a report to the French people justifying the expulsion of 29 Girondins. Later 120 deputies who signed a protest against the purge were themselves suspended from the convention, and in October the original Girondins stood trial before the Revolutionary Tribunal, which sentenced them to death. The Montagnard ascendancy had begun.

Though the deadlock in the convention was now broken, the balance of forces in the country was by no means clear. The Parisian sansculottes might well have continued to intimidate the convention and emerge as the dominant partner in their alliance with the Montagnards—just as Girondin orators had warned. Conversely, provincial opinion might have rebelled against this mutilation of the National Convention by Paris and its Montagnard partisans. Purged of the Girondins, the Convention itself was able to reach consensus more readily, but the nation as a whole was more divided than ever.

At first it seemed as if the expulsion of the Girondins would indeed backfire. More than half of the departmental directories protested against the purge. But, faced with pleas for unity and threats from the convention, most of this opposition subsided quickly. Only 13 *départements* continued their defiant stance, and only 6 of these passed into overt armed rebellion against the Convention's authority. Still, this was a serious threat in a country already beleaguered by civil war and military reversals. The Jacobins stigmatized this new opposition as the heresy of federalism—implying that the "federalists" no longer believed in a unified republic. Jacobin propaganda depicted the federalists as counterrevolutionaries. In fact, most were moderate republicans hostile to the royalists and committed to constitutional liberties. They did not intend to overthrow the republic or separate from it. Rather they hoped to wrest power back from what they deemed the tyrannical alliance of Montagnards and Parisian sansculottes.

THE FRENCH REVOLUTION, NAPOLEON, AND THE REPUBLIC:
LIBERTÉ, ÉGALITÉ, AND FRATERNITÉ

In Lyon, Marseille, Toulon, and Bordeaux, bitter conflicts between local moderates and Jacobins contributed decisively to the rebellion. Uprisings in Lyon and Marseille (France's second- and third-largest cities, respectively) began in late May when moderates seized power from local Jacobin authorities who had threatened their lives and property—Jacobins such as the firebrand Marie-Joseph Chalier in Lyon, who was supported by Montagnard representatives-on-mission. The expulsion of the Girondins was merely the last straw. Whatever its causes, however, "federalist" rebellion did threaten national unity and the convention's sovereign authority. Royalists, moreover, did gain control of the movement in Toulon and opened that port to the British. Holding out no offer of negotiation, the convention organized military force to crush the rebellions and promised the leaders exemplary punishment. "Lyon has made war against liberty," declared the convention, "Lyon no longer exists." When the republic's forces recaptured the city in October, they changed its name to Liberated City, demolished the houses of the wealthy, and summarily executed more than 2,000 Lyonnais, including many wealthy merchants.

THE REIGN OF TERROR

After their victory in expelling the Girondins, Parisian militants "regenerated" their own sectional assemblies by purging local moderates, while radicals such as Jacques-René Hébert and Pierre-Gaspard Chaumette tightened their grip on the Paris Commune. On September 5, 1793, they mounted another mass demonstration to demand that the Convention assure food at affordable prices and "place terror on the order of the day." Led by its Committee of Public Safety, the convention placated the popular movement with decisive actions. It proclaimed the need for terror against the Revolution's enemies, made economic crimes such as hoarding into capital offenses, and decreed a system of price and wage controls known as the Maximum. The Law of Suspects empowered local revolutionary committees to arrest "those who by their conduct, relations or language spoken or written, have shown themselves partisans of tyranny or federalism and enemies of liberty." In 1793–94 well over 200,000 citizens were detained under this law; though most of them never stood trial, they languished in pestiferous jails, where an estimated 10,000 perished. About 17,000 death sentences were handed down by the military commissions and revolutionary tribunals of the Terror, 72 percent for charges of armed rebellion in the two major zones of civil war—the federalist southeast and the western Vendée region. One-third of the *départements*, however, had fewer than 10 death sentences passed on their inhabitants and were relatively tranquil.

To help police the Maximum and requisition grain in the countryside, as well as to carry out arrest warrants and guard political prisoners, the Convention authorized local authorities to create paramilitary forces. About 50 such *armées révolutionnaires* came into being as ambulatory instruments of the Terror in the provinces. Fraternizing with peasants and artisans in the hinterland, these forces helped raise revolutionary enthusiasm but ultimately left such village sansculottes vulnerable to the wrath of the wealthy citizens whom they harassed.

Back in June the convention had quickly drafted a new democratic constitution, incorporating such popular demands as universal male suffrage, the right to subsistence, and the right to free public education. In a referendum this Jacobin constitution

THE FRENCH REVOLUTION, NAPOLEON, AND THE REPUBLIC:
LIBERTÉ, ÉGALITÉ, AND FRATERNITÉ

of 1793 was approved virtually without dissent by about two million voters. Because of the emergency, however, the Convention placed the new constitution on the shelf in October and declared that "the provisional government of France is revolutionary until the peace." There would be no elections, no local autonomy, no guarantees of individual liberties for the duration of the emergency. The convention would rule with a sovereignty more absolute than the old monarchy had ever claimed. Nor would serious popular protest be tolerated any longer, now that the Jacobins had used such intervention to secure power. The balance in the alliance between Montagnards and sansculottes gradually shifted from the streets of Paris to the halls and committee rooms of the convention.

From the beginning a popular terrorist mentality had helped shape the Revolution. Peasants and townspeople alike had been galvanized by fear and rage over "aristocratic plots" in 1789. Lynchings of "enemies of the people" punctuated the Revolution, culminating in the September massacres, which reflected an extreme fear of betrayal and an unbridled punitive will. Now the Revolution's leaders were preempting this punitive will in order to control it: they conceived of terror as rational rather than emotional and as organized rather than instinctive. Paradoxically they were trying to render terror lawful—legality being an article of faith among most revolutionaries—but without the procedural safeguards that accompanied the regular criminal code of 1791.

For the more pragmatic Montagnards that deviation was justified by the unparalleled emergency situation confronting France in 1793: before the benefits of the Revolution could be enjoyed, they must be secured against their enemies by force. ("Terror is nothing other than justice, prompt, severe, inflexible…

THE FIRST FRENCH REPUBLIC

The last prisoners awaiting execution during the Reign of Terror in 1794, undated engraving.

Is force made only to protect crime?" declared Robespierre.) For the more ideologically exalted Jacobins such as Robespierre and Louis de Saint-Just, however, the Terror would also regenerate the nation by promoting equality and the public interest. In their minds a link existed between terror and virtue: "virtue, without which terror is fatal; terror, without which virtue is powerless." Whoever could claim to speak for the interests of the people held the mantle of virtue and the power of revolutionary terror.

THE FRENCH REVOLUTION, NAPOLEON, AND THE REPUBLIC:
LIBERTÉ, ÉGALITÉ, AND FRATERNITÉ

THE JACOBIN DICTATORSHIP

One of the changes affected by the convention was the creation of the French republican calendar to replace the Gregorian calendar, which was viewed as nonscientific and tainted with religious associations. The Revolutionary calendar was proclaimed on 14 Vendémiaire, year II (October 5, 1793), but its starting point was set to be about a year prior, on 1 Vendémiaire, year I (September 22, 1792). The new calendar featured a 10-day week called the *décade*, designed to swallow up the Christian Sunday in a new cycle of work and recreation. Three *décades* formed a month of 30 days, and 12 months formed a year, with 5 to 6 additional days at the end of each year.

The convention consolidated its revolutionary government in the Law of 14 Frimaire, year II (December 4, 1793). To organize the Revolution, to promote confidence and

FRENCH REPUBLICAN CALENDAR

The French republican calendar was a dating system adopted in 1793 during the French Revolution that was intended to replace the Gregorian calendar with a more scientific and rational system that would avoid Christian associations. The Revolutionary Convention established the calendar on October 5, 1793, setting its beginning (1 Vendémiaire, year I) to a date nearly a year prior (September 22, 1792), when the National Convention had proclaimed France a republic.

The French republican calendar was based on a secular calendar first presented by Pierre-Sylvain Maréchal in 1788. The 12 months of the calendar each contained three *décades* (instead of weeks) of 10 days each; at the end of the year were grouped five (six in leap years) supplementary days. The months in order—beginning with one corresponding to the Gregorian months of September and October—were Vendémiaire (meaning "vintage"), Brumaire ("mist"), Frimaire ("frost"), Nivôse ("snow"), Pluviôse ("rain"), Ventôse ("wind"), Germinal ("seedtime"), Floréal ("blossom"), Prairial ("meadow"), Messidor ("harvest"), Thermidor ("heat"), and Fructidor ("fruits"). The names were the invention of poet Philippe Fabre d'Églantine. Each of the 360 days in the year was named for a seed, tree, flower, fruit, animal, or tool, replacing the saints'-day names and Christian festivals.

Among the notable historical events marked by the republican calendar were the consolidation of the Revolutionary government on 14 Frimaire, year II (December 4, 1793), legislation that accelerated the Reign of Terror on 22 Prairial, year II (June 10, 1794), the arrest of Robespierre and the Thermidor Reaction on 9 Thermidor, year II (July 27, 1794), the insurrection of the sansculottes on 1 Prairial, year III (May 20, 1795), and the various coups d'état that marked the ascendancy of the directory and then of Napoleon on 18 Fructidor, year V (September 4, 1797), 30 Prairial, year VII (June 18, 1799), and 18 Brumaire, year VIII (November 9, 1799).

The Gregorian calendar was reestablished in France when the republican calendar was abandoned by the Napoleonic regime on January 1, 1806.

compliance, efficiency and control, this law centralized authority in a parliamentary dictatorship, with the Committee of Public Safety at the helm. The committee already controlled military policy and patronage; henceforth local administrators (renamed national agents), tribunals, and revolutionary committees also came under its scrutiny and control. The network of Jacobin clubs was enlisted to monitor

THE FRENCH REVOLUTION, NAPOLEON, AND THE REPUBLIC:
LIBERTÉ, ÉGALITÉ, AND FRATERNITÉ

local officials, nominate new appointees, and in general serve as "arsenals of public opinion."

Opposed to "ultrarevolutionary" behaviour and uncoordinated actions even by its own deputies-on-mission, the committee tried to stop the de-Christianization campaigns that had erupted during the anarchic phase of the Terror in the fall of 1793. Usually instigated by radical deputies, the de-Christianizers vandalized churches or closed them down altogether, intimidated constitutional priests into resigning their vocation, and often pressured them into marrying to demonstrate the sincerity of their conversion. Favouring a deistic form of civil religion, Robespierre implied that the atheism displayed by some de-Christianizers was a variant of counterrevolution. He insisted that citizens must be left free to practice the Roman Catholic religion, though for the time being most priests were not holding services.

The committee also felt strong enough a few months later to curb the activism of the Paris sections, dissolve the *armées révolutionnaires*, and purge the Paris Commune—ironically what the Girondins had hoped to do months before. But in this atmosphere no serious dissent to official policy was tolerated. The once vibrant free press had been muzzled after the purge of the Girondins. In March 1794 Hébert and other "ultrarevolutionaries" were arrested, sent to the Revolutionary Tribunal, and guillotined. A month later Danton and other so-called indulgents met the same fate for seeking to end the Terror—prematurely in the eyes of the committee. Then the convention passed the infamous law of 22 Prairial, year II (June 10, 1794), to streamline revolutionary justice, denying the accused any effective right to self-defense and eliminating all sentences other than acquittal or death. Indictments by the public prosecutor, now virtually tantamount to a death sentence, multiplied rapidly.

THE FIRST FRENCH REPUBLIC

The Terror was being escalated just when danger no longer threatened the republic—after French armies had prevailed against Austria at the decisive Battle of Fleurus on 8 Messidor (June 26) and long after rebel forces in the Vendée, Lyon, and elsewhere had been vanquished. By that time the Jacobin dictatorship had forged an effective government and had mobilized the nation's resources, thereby mastering the crisis that had brought it into being. Yet, on 8 Thermidor (July 26), Robespierre took the rostrum to proclaim his own probity and to denounce yet another unnamed group as traitors hatching "a conspiracy

ROBESPIERRE IS ARRESTED DURING THE THERMIDORIAN REACTION AND, LATER, EXECUTED, UNDATED PRINT.

THE FRENCH REVOLUTION, NAPOLEON, AND THE REPUBLIC:
LIBERTÉ, ÉGALITÉ, AND FRATERNITÉ

against liberty." Robespierre had clearly lost his grip on reality in his obsession with national unity and virtue. An awkward coalition of moderates, Jacobin pragmatists, rival deputies, and extremists who rightly felt threatened by the Incorruptible (as he was known) finally combined to topple Robespierre and his closest followers. On 9 Thermidor, year II (July 27, 1794), the convention ordered the arrest of Robespierre and Saint-Just, and, after a failed resistance by loyalists in the Paris Commune, they were guillotined without trial the following day. The Terror was over.

THE ARMY OF THE REPUBLIC

The Jacobin dictatorship had been an unstable blend of exalted patriotism, resolute political leadership, ideological fanaticism, and populist initiatives. The rhetoric and symbolism of democracy constituted a new civic pedagogy, matched by bold egalitarian policies. The army was a primary focal point of this democratic impetus. In 1790 the National Assembly had opted for a small military of long-term professionals. One-year volunteers bolstered the line army after the outbreak of war, and in March 1793 the Convention called for an additional 300,000 soldiers, with quotas to be provided by each *département*. Finally, in August 1793 it decreed the *levée en masse*—a "requisition" of all able-bodied, unmarried men between the ages of 18 and 25. Despite massive draft evasion and desertion, within a year almost three-quarters of a million men were under arms, the citizen-soldiers merged with line-army troops in new units called *demibrigades*. This huge popular mobilization reinforced the Revolution's militant spirit. The citizen-soldiers risking their lives at the front had to be supported by any and all means back home, including forced loans on the rich and punitive vigilance against those suspected of disloyalty.

Within the constraints of military discipline, the army became a model of democratic practice. Both noncommissioned and commissioned officers were chosen by a combination of election and appointment, in which seniority received some consideration, but demonstrated talent on the battlefield brought the most rapid promotion. The republic insisted that officers be respectful toward their men and share their privations. Jacobin military prosecutors enforced the laws against insubordination and desertion but took great pains to explain them to the soldiers and to make allowances for momentary weakness in deciding cases. Soldiers received revolutionary newspapers and sang revolutionary songs, exalting the citizen-soldier as the model sansculotte. Meanwhile, needy parents, wives, or dependents of soldiers at the front received subsidies, while common soldiers seriously wounded in action earned extremely generous veterans' benefits.

The Revolution's egalitarian promise never involved an assault on private property, but its concept of "social limitations" on property made it possible for the convention to abolish all seigneurial dues without compensation, abolish slavery in the colonies (where slave rebellions had already achieved that result in practice), endorse the idea of progressive taxation, and temporarily regulate the economy in favour of consumers. In 1793–94 the Convention enacted an unprecedented national system of public assistance entitlements, with one program allocating small pensions to poor families with dependent children and another providing pensions to aged and indigent farm workers, artisans,

THE FRENCH REVOLUTION, NAPOLEON, AND THE REPUBLIC:
LIBERTÉ, ÉGALITÉ, AND FRATERNITÉ

and rural widows—the neediest of the needy. "We must put an end to the servitude of the most basic needs, the slavery of misery, that most hideous of inequalities," declared Barère of the Committee of Public Safety. The convention also implemented the Revolution's long-standing commitment to primary education with a system of free public primary schooling for both boys and girls. The Lakanal Law of November 1794 authorized public schools in every commune with more than 1,000 inhabitants, the teachers to be selected by examination and paid fixed salaries by the government.

THE THERMIDORIAN REACTION

With control passing from the Montagnards after Robespierre's fall, moderates in the convention hoped to put the Terror and sansculotte militance behind them while standing fast against counterrevolution and rallying all patriots around the original principles of the Revolution. But far from stabilizing the Revolution, the fall of "the tyrant" on 9 Thermidor set in motion a brutal struggle for power. Those who had suffered under the Terror now clamoured for retribution, and moderation quickly gave way to reaction. As federalists were released, Jacobins were arrested; as the suspended Girondins were reinstated, Montagnards were purged; as moderates could feel safe, Jacobins and sansculottes were threatened. Like the Terror, the Thermidorian Reaction had an uncontrollable momentum of its own. Antiterrorism—in the press, the theatre, the streets—degenerated into a "white terror" against the men of year II. In the south, especially in Provence and the Rhône valley, the frontier between private feuds and political reaction blurred as law and order broke down. Accounts were settled by lynchings, murder gangs, and prison massacres of arrested sansculottes.

In addition to these political consequences, the Thermidorian Reaction set off a new economic and monetary crisis. Committed to free-trade principles, the Thermidorians dismantled the economic regulation and price controls of year II, along with the apparatus of the Terror that had put teeth into that system. The depreciation of the assignats, which the Terror had halted, quickly resumed. By 1795 the cities were desperately short of grain and flour, while meat, fuel, dairy products, and soap were entirely beyond the reach of ordinary consumers. By the spring of 1795 scarcity was turning into famine for working people of the capital and other cities. Surviving cadres of sansculottes in the Paris sections mobilized to halt the reaction and the economic catastrophe it had unleashed. After trying petitions and demonstrations, a crowd of sansculottes invaded the Convention on 1 Prairial, year III (May 20, 1795), in the last popular uprising of the French Revolution. "Bread is the goal of their insurrection, physically speaking," reported a police observer, "but the Constitution of 1793 is its soul." This rearguard rebellion of despair was doomed to fail, despite the support of a few remaining Montagnard deputies, whose fraternization with the demonstrators was to cost them their lives after the insurgents were routed the following day.

Instead of implementing the democratic Constitution of 1793, the Thermidorian Convention was preparing a new, more conservative charter. Anti-Jacobin and antiroyalist, the Thermidorians clung to the elusive centre of the political spectrum. Their Constitution of Year III (1795) established a liberal republic with a franchise based on the payment of taxes similar to that of 1791, a two-house legislature to slow down the

THE FRENCH REVOLUTION, NAPOLEON, AND THE REPUBLIC:
LIBERTÉ, ÉGALITÉ, AND FRATERNITÉ

legislative process, and a five-man executive directory to be chosen by the legislature. Within a liberal framework, the central government retained great power, including emergency powers to curb freedom of the press and freedom of association. Departmental and municipal administrators were to be elected but could be removed by the directory, and commissioners appointed by the directory were to monitor them and report on their compliance with the laws.

THE DIRECTORY

The new regime, referred to as the Directory, began auspiciously in October 1795 with a successful constitutional plebiscite and a general amnesty for political prisoners. But as one of its final acts the convention added the "Two-Thirds Decree" to the package, requiring for the sake of continuity that two-thirds of its deputies must sit by right in the new legislature regardless of voting in the *départements*. This outraged conservatives and royalists hoping to regain power legally, but their armed uprising in Paris was easily suppressed by the army. The Directory also weathered a conspiracy on the far left by a cabal of unreconciled militants organized around a program of communistic equality and revolutionary dictatorship. The Babeuf plot was exposed in May 1796 by a police spy, and a lengthy trial ensued in which François-Noël ("Gracchus") Babeuf, the self-styled "Tribune of the People," was sentenced to death.

Apart from these conspiracies, the political life of the Directory revolved around annual elections to replace one-third of the deputies and local administrators. The spirit of the Two-Thirds Decree haunted this process, however, since the directors believed that stability required their continuation in

FRANÇOIS-NOËL BABEUF

François-Noël Babeuf (born November 23, 1760, Saint-Quentin, France—died May 27, 1797, Vendôme) was an early political journalist and agitator in Revolutionary France whose tactical strategies provided a model for left-wing movements of the 19th century and who was called Gracchus for the resemblance of his proposed agrarian reforms to those of the 2nd-century-BC Roman statesman of that name.

Following an arrest and brief imprisonment in 1790, Babeuf founded a journal, *Le Correspondant picard*, in which he advocated a program of radical agrarian reforms. They included the abolition of feudal dues and the redistribution of land. During this period he served as an administrator in the Montdidier district of the Somme, but in February 1793 he returned to Paris, where, during the Reign of Terror, he was again arrested and imprisoned. After his release following Robespierre's fall in July 1794, he founded a new journal, *Le Journal de la liberté de la presse* (shortly thereafter renamed *Le Tribun du peuple*), in which he at first defended the Thermidorians and attacked the Jacobins. When he began to attack the Thermidorians, he was again arrested (February 12, 1795) and imprisoned at Arras.

During this brief imprisonment, Babeuf continued to formulate his egalitarian doctrines, advocating an equal distribution of land and income, and after his release he began a career as a professional revolutionary. He quickly rose to a position of leadership in the Society of the Pantheon, which sought political and economic equality in defiance of the new French Constitution of 1795. After the society was dissolved in 1796, he founded a "secret directory of public safety" to plan an insurrection.

On May 8, 1796, a general meeting of Babouvist, Jacobin, and military insurrectionary committees took place in order to plan the

THE FRENCH REVOLUTION, NAPOLEON, AND THE REPUBLIC:
LIBERTÉ, ÉGALITÉ, AND FRATERNITÉ

raising of a force of 17,000 men to overthrow the Directory and to institute a return to the Constitution of 1793, which the committee members considered the document most legitimately sanctioned by popular deliberation. On May 10, however, the conspirators were arrested after an informant revealed their plans to the government. The trial took place between February 20 and May 26, 1797. All conspirators were acquitted except Babeuf and his companion, Augustin Darthé, both of whom were guillotined.

Babeuf was revered as a hero by 19th- and 20th-century revolutionaries because of his advocacy of communism and his conviction that a small elite could overthrow an undesirable government by conspiratorial means.

power and the exclusion of royalists or Jacobins. The Directory would tolerate no organized opposition. During or immediately after each election, the government in effect violated the constitution in order to save it, whenever the right or the left seemed to be gaining ground.

As a legacy of the nation's revolutionary upheavals, elections under the Directory displayed an unhealthy combination of massive apathy and rancorous partisanship by small minorities. When the elections of 1797 produced a royalist resurgence, the government responded with the coup of Fructidor, year V (September 1797), ousting two of the current directors, arresting leading royalist politicians, annulling the elections in 49 *départements*, shutting down the royalist press, and resuming the vigorous pursuit of returned émigrés and refractory clergy. This heartened the Neo-Jacobins, who organized new clubs called constitutional circles to emphasize their adherence to the regime. But this independent political activism on the left raised the spectre of 1793 for the Directory, and in turn it closed down the Neo-Jacobin clubs and newspapers, warned citizens against voting for "anarchists" in the elections of 1798, and promoted schisms in electoral assemblies when voters spurned this advice. When democrats (or Neo-Jacobins) prevailed nonetheless, the Directory organized another purge in the coup of Floréal, year VI (May 1798), by annulling all or some elections in 29 *départements*. Ambivalent and fainthearted in its republican commitment, the Directory was eroding political liberty from within. But as long as the Constitution of 1795 endured, it remained possible that political liberty and free elections might one day take root.

SISTER REPUBLICS

Meanwhile the Directory regime successfully exported revolution abroad by helping to create "sister republics" in western Europe. During the Revolution's most radical phase, in 1793–94, French expansion had stopped more or less at the nation's self-proclaimed "natural frontiers"—the Rhine, Alps, and Pyrenees. The Austrian Netherlands (now Belgium) and the left bank of the Rhine had been major battlefields in the war against the coalition, and French victories in those sectors were followed by military occupation, requisitions, and taxation but also by the abolition of feudalism and similar reforms. In 1795 Belgium was annexed to France and divided into departments, which would henceforth be treated like other French *départements*.

THE FRENCH REVOLUTION, NAPOLEON, AND THE REPUBLIC:
LIBERTÉ, ÉGALITÉ, AND FRATERNITÉ

Strategic considerations and French national interest were the main engines of French foreign policy in the Revolutionary decade but not the only ones. Elsewhere in Europe, native patriots invited French support against their own ruling princes or oligarchies. Europe was divided not simply by a conflict between Revolutionary France and other states but by conflicts within various states between revolutionary or democratic forces and conservative or traditional forces. Indeed, abortive revolutionary movements had already occurred in the Austrian Netherlands and in the United Provinces (Dutch Netherlands). When French troops occupied their country in 1795, Dutch "Patriots" set up the Batavian Republic, the first of what became a belt of "sister republics" along France's borders.

By 1797 Prussia and Spain had made peace with France, but Austria and Britain continued the struggle. In 1796 the French had launched an attack across the Alps aimed at Habsburg Lombardy, from which they hoped to drive north toward Vienna. Commanded by General Napoleon Bonaparte, this campaign succeeded beyond expectations. In the process, northern Italy was liberated from Austria, and the Habsburgs were driven to the peace table, where they signed the Treaty of Campo Formio on 26 Vendémiaire, year VI (October 17, 1797). Italian revolutionaries under French protection proclaimed the Cisalpine Republic in northern Italy, later joined by the Helvetic Republic in Switzerland, and two very shaky republics—the Roman Republic in central Italy and the Parthenopean Republic in the south around Naples. All these republics were exploited financially by the French, but then again their survival depended on the costly presence of French troops. The French interfered in their internal politics, but this was no more than the Directory was doing at home. Because these republics could

THE FIRST FRENCH REPUBLIC

Napoleon is given the presidency by the Council of the Cisalpine Republic, one of several puppet states proclaimed by Napoleon-supported revolutionaries in territories bordering France; painting by Nicolas Mansiaux, 19th century.

not defend themselves in isolation, they acted like sponges on French resources as much as they provided treasure or other benefits to France. France's extended lines of occupation made it extremely vulnerable to attack when Britain organized a second coalition in 1798 that included Russia and Austria. But when the battles were over, Switzerland, northern Italy, and the Netherlands remained in the French sphere of influence.

The treasure coming from the sister republics was desperately needed in Paris since French finances were in total

THE FRENCH REVOLUTION, NAPOLEON, AND THE REPUBLIC:
LIBERTÉ, EGALITÉ, AND FRATERNITÉ

disarray. The collapse of the assignats and the hyperinflation of 1795–96 not only destroyed such social programs as public assistance pensions and free public schooling but also strained the regime's capacity to keep its basic institutions running. In 1797 the government finally engineered a painful return to hard currency and in effect wrote down the accumulated national debt by two-thirds of its value in exchange for guaranteeing the integrity of the remaining third.

ALIENATION AND COUPS

After the Fructidor coup of 1797 the Directory imprudently resumed the republic's assault on the Roman Catholic religion. Besides prohibiting the outward signs of Catholicism, such as the ringing of church bells or the display of crosses, the government revived the Revolutionary calendar, which had fallen into disuse after the Thermidorian Reaction. The Directory ordered in 1798 that *décadi* (the final day of the 10-day week, or *décade*) be treated as the official day of rest for workers and businesses as well as public employees and schoolchildren. Forbidding organized recreation on Sundays, the regime also pressured Catholic priests to celebrate Mass on *décadis* rather than on ex-Sundays. This aggressive confrontation with the habits and beliefs of most French citizens sapped whatever shreds of popularity the regime still had.

French citizens were already alienated by the Directory's foreign policy and its new conscription law. Conscription became a permanent obligation of young men between the ages of 20 and 25 under the Jourdan Law of 19 Fructidor, year VI (September 5, 1798), named for its sponsor, the comte de

Jourdan. To fight the War of the Second Coalition that began in 1799, the Directory mobilized three "classes," or age cohorts, of young men but encountered massive draft resistance and desertion in many regions. Meanwhile, retreating armies in the field lacked rations and supplies because, it was alleged, corrupt military contractors operated in collusion with government officials. This war crisis prompted the legislature to oust four of the directors in the coup on 30 Prairial, year VII (June 18, 1799), and allowed a brief resurgence of Neo-Jacobin agitation for drastic emergency measures.

In reality the balance of power was swinging toward a group of disaffected conservatives. Led by Sieyès, one of the new directors, these "revisionists" wished to escape from the instability of the Directory regime, especially its tumultuous annual elections and its cumbersome separation of powers. They wanted a more reliable structure of political power, which would allow the new elite to govern securely and thereby guarantee the basic reforms and property rights of 1789. Ironically, the Neo-Jacobins stood as the constitution's most ardent defenders against the maneuvers of these "oligarchs."

Using mendacious allegations about Neo-Jacobin plots as a cover, the revisionists prepared a parliamentary coup to jettison the constitution. To provide the necessary military insurance, the plotters sought a leading general. Though he was not their first choice, they eventually enlisted Napoleon—recently returned from his Egyptian campaign, about whose disasters the public knew almost nothing. Given a central role in the coup, which occurred on 18 Brumaire, year VIII (November 9, 1799), General Bonaparte addressed the legislature, and, when some

THE FRENCH REVOLUTION, NAPOLEON, AND THE REPUBLIC:
LIBERTÉ, EGALITÉ, AND FRATERNITÉ

deputies balked at his call for scrapping the constitution, his troopers cleared the hall. A rump of each house then convened to draft a new constitution, and during these deliberations Napoleon shouldered aside Sieyès and emerged as the dominant figure in the new regime. The Brumaire event was not really a military coup and did not at first produce a dictatorship. It was a parliamentary coup to create a new constitution and was welcomed by people of differing opinions who saw in it what they wished to see. The image of an energetic military hero impatient with the abuses of the past must have seemed reassuring.

THE NAPOLEONIC ERA

The revisionists who engineered the Brumaire coup intended to create a strong, elitist government that would curb the republic's political turmoil and guarantee the conquests of 1789. They had in mind what might be called a senatorial oligarchy rather than a personal dictatorship. General Bonaparte, however, advocated a more drastic concentration of power. Within days of the coup, Napoleon emerged as the dominant figure, an insistent and persuasive presence who inspired confidence. Clearly outmaneuvered, Sieyès soon withdrew from the scene, taking with him his complex notions of checks and balances. While the regime, known as the Consulate, maintained a republican form, Napoleon became from its inception a new kind of authoritarian leader.

THE FRENCH REVOLUTION, NAPOLEON, AND THE REPUBLIC:
LIBERTÉ, ÉGALITÉ, AND FRATERNITÉ

THE CONSULATE

Approved almost unanimously in a plebiscite by 3,000,000 votes (of which half may have been manufactured out of thin air), the Constitution of the Year VIII created an executive consisting of three consuls, but the first consul wielded all real power. That office was, of course, vested in Napoleon. In 1802, after a string of military and diplomatic victories, another plebiscite endowed him with the position for life. By 1804 Napoleon's grip on power was complete, and belief in his indispensability was pervasive in the governing class. In April 1804 various government bodies agreed "that Napoleon Bonaparte be declared Emperor and that the imperial dignity be declared hereditary in his family." The Constitution of the Year XII (May 1804), establishing the empire, was approved in a plebiscite by more than 3,500,000 votes against about 2,500. (After this point General Bonaparte was known officially as Emperor Napoleon I.)

The Constitution of 1791, the convention, and the Directory alike had been organized around representation and legislative supremacy, the fundamental political principles first proclaimed in June 1789 by the National Assembly. This tradition came to an end with the Consulate. Its new bicameral legislature lost the power to initiate legislation; now the executive branch drafted new laws. One house (the Tribunate) debated such proposals, either endorsed or opposed them, and then sent deputies to present its opinion to the other house, the Corps Législatif, which also heard from government spokesmen. Without the right to debate, the Corps Législatif then voted on whether to enact the bill. Even these limited powers were rarely used independently, since both houses were appointed in the first instance by the government

THE NAPOLEONIC ERA

First Consul Bonaparte, oil on canvas by Antoine-Jean Gros, c. 1802; National Museum of the Legion of Honor, Paris.

THE FRENCH REVOLUTION, NAPOLEON, AND THE REPUBLIC:
LIBERTÉ, ÉGALITÉ, AND FRATERNITÉ

and later renewed by co-option. When certain tribunes such as Benjamin Constant did manifest a critical spirit, they were eventually purged, and in 1807 the Tribunate was suppressed altogether. On the whole, then, the legislative branch of government became little more than a rubber stamp.

After the Brumaire coup, Sieyès had envisaged an independent institution called the Senate to conserve the constitution by interpreting it in the light of changing circumstances. In practice, the Senate became the handmaiden of Napoleon's expanding authority, sanctioning changes such as the life consulship, the purge of the Tribunate, and Napoleon's elevation to the rank of hereditary emperor. For creating "legislation above the laws" at Napoleon's behest, its 80 handpicked members were opulently rewarded with money and honours. As power shifted decisively to the executive branch, Napoleon enlisted a new institution called the Conseil d'État (Council of State) to formulate policy, draft legislation, and supervise the ministries. Appointed by the first consul, this body of experienced jurists and legislators was drawn from across the former political spectrum. Talent and loyalty to the new government were the relevant criteria for these coveted posts.

The Consulate did not entirely eliminate the electoral principle from the new regime, but voters were left with no real power, and elections became an elaborate charade. Citizens voted only for electoral colleges, which in turn created lists of candidates from which the government might fill occasional vacancies in

The institution of the Conseil d'État still exists to this day, housed in the Palais-Royal in Paris, France.

the Conseil d'État or Senate. In the event, the primary assemblies of voters were rarely convened, and membership in the electoral colleges became a kind of honorific lifetime position. The judiciary, too, lost its elective status. In the hope of creating a more professional and compliant judiciary, the Consulate's sweeping judicial reform provided for lifetime appointments of judges—which did not prevent Napoleon from purging the judiciary in 1808. Napoleon was also disposed to eliminate criminal juries as well, but the Conseil d'État prevailed on him to maintain them.

Successive Revolutionary regimes had always balanced local elections with central control, but the Consulate destroyed that balance completely. The Local Government Act of February 1800 eliminated elections for local office entirely and organized local administration from the top down. To

THE FRENCH REVOLUTION, NAPOLEON, AND THE REPUBLIC:
LIBERTÉ, ÉGALITÉ, AND FRATERNITÉ

run each *département*, the Consulate appointed a prefect, reminiscent of the old royal intendants, who was assisted by subprefects on the level of the arrondissements (subdistricts of the *départements*) and by appointed mayors in each commune. The original Revolutionary commitment to local autonomy gave way before the rival principles of centralization and uniformity. The prefect became the cornerstone of the Napoleonic dictatorship, supervising local government at all levels, keeping careful watch over his *département*'s "public spirit," and above all assuring that taxes and conscripts flowed in smoothly. While even the most trivial local matter had to be referred to the prefect, all major decisions taken by the prefect had in turn to be sanctioned by the interior ministry in Paris.

LOSS OF POLITICAL FREEDOM

Politics during the Directory had been marked by an unwholesome combination of ferocious partisanship and massive apathy. Weary of political turmoil and disillusioned by politicians of all kinds, most Frenchmen now accepted the disappearance of political freedom and participation with equanimity. The few who still cared passionately enough to resist collided with the apparatus of a police state. A regime that entirely avoided genuine elections would scarcely permit open political dissent. Where the Directory had been ambivalent about freedom of association, for example, the Consulate simply banned political clubs outright and placed Jacobin and royalist cadres under surveillance by the police ministry. In 1801, blaming democratic militants for a botched attempt to assassinate him with a bomb as his carriage drove down the rue Saint-Nicaise—a plot actually hatched by fanatical royalists—Napoleon ordered the arrest and deportation to Guiana of about 100 former Jacobin and sansculotte militants. In 1804 he had the duc d'Enghien, a member of the Bourbon family, abducted from abroad, convicted of conspiracy by a court-martial, and executed.

Outspoken liberals also felt the lash of Napoleon's intolerance for any kind of opposition. After he purged the Tribunate, the consul registered his displeasure with the salon politics of liberal intellectuals by dissolving the Class of Moral and Political Science of the National Institute in 1803. One of the most principled liberals, Madame de Staël, chose to go into exile rather than exercise the self-censorship demanded by the regime. Meanwhile, the only newspapers tolerated were heavily censored. Paris, for example, had more than 70 newspapers at the time of the Brumaire coup; by 1811 only four quasi-official newspapers survived, ironically the same number as had existed before 1789. In the provinces each *département* had at most one newspaper, likewise of quasi-official character. The reimposition of censorship was matched by Napoleon's astute management of news and propaganda.

SOCIETY IN NAPOLEONIC FRANCE

The Consulate's work of administrative reform, undertaken at Napoleon's instigation, was to be more lasting than its constitution and so more important for France. Even more enduring, however,

THE FRENCH REVOLUTION, NAPOLEON, AND THE REPUBLIC:
LIBERTÉ, ÉGALITÉ, AND FRATERNITÉ

were its social reforms, which helped solidify the achievements of the Revolution and ease tensions among the different sectors of French society.

Education was transformed into a major public service; secondary education was given a semimilitary organization, and the university faculties were reestablished. (Primary education, however, was still neglected.) In terms of religious life, it was Napoleon's belief that the people needed a religion and religious peace had to be restored to France. In 1801 negotiations with the recently elected Pope Pius VII would reconcile the church and the Revolution. Perhaps most important the codification of the civil law, first undertaken in 1790, was at last completed under the Consulate.

RELIGIOUS POLICY

If the Consulate's motto was "Authority from above, confidence from below," Napoleon's religious policy helped secure that confidence. The concordat negotiated with the papacy in 1801 reintegrated the Roman Catholic Church into French society and ended the cycle of bare toleration and persecution that had begun in 1792. Having immediately halted the campaign to enforce the republican calendar (which was quietly abolished on January 1, 1806), the Consulate then extended an olive branch to the refractory clergy. The state continued to respect the religious freedom of non-Catholics, but the concordat recognized Catholicism as "the preferred religion" of France—in effect, though not in name, the nation's established religion. Upkeep of the church became a significant item in local budgets, and the clergy regained de facto control over primary education. The state, however, retained the

THE NAPOLEONIC ERA

Portrait of Pope Pius VII painted by unknown artist, 19th century.

THE FRENCH REVOLUTION, NAPOLEON, AND THE REPUBLIC:
LIBERTÉ, ÉGALITÉ, AND FRATERNITÉ

upper hand in church-state relations. By signing the concordat, the pope accepted the nationalization of church property in France and its sale as *biens nationaux*. Bishops, though again consecrated by Rome, were named by the head of state, and the government retained the right to police public worship.

The most conservative Catholics looked askance at the concordat, which in their eyes promoted an excessively national or Gallican church rather than a truly Roman Catholic Church. They correctly suspected that Napoleon—personally a religious skeptic—would use it as a tool of his own ambitions. Indeed, he claimed that the clergy would become his "moral prefects," propagating traditional values and obedience to authority. Later, for example, the clergy was asked to teach an imperial catechism, which would "bind the consciences of the young to the august person of the Emperor."

The Napoleonic regime also organized France's approximately 1,000,000 Calvinists into hierarchical "consistories" subject to oversight by the state. Protestant pastors, paid by the state, were designated by the elders who led local congregations and consistories; the more democratic tendencies of Calvinism were thus weakened in exchange for official recognition. France's 60,000 Jews, residing mainly in Alsace and Lorraine, were also organized into consistories. Like priests and pastors, their rabbis were enlisted to promote obedience to the laws, though they were not salaried by the state. Napoleon's convocation in 1807 of a "Grand Sanhedrin" of Jewish religious authorities to reconcile French and Jewish law attracted widespread attention. Official recognition, however, did not prevent discriminatory measures against Jews. A law of 1808, ostensibly for "the social reformation of the Jews," appeased peasant debtors in Alsace by canceling their debts to Jewish moneylenders.

THE NAPOLEONIC ERA

NAPOLEONIC NOBILITY

Napoleon cultivated the loyalty of the nation's wealthy landed proprietors by a system of patronage and honours. He thereby facilitated the emergence of a ruling class drawn from both the middle classes and the nobility of the old regime, which had been divided by the artificial barriers of old-regime estates and privileges. The principal artifacts of Napoleon's social policy were the lists he ordered of the 600 highest-paid taxpayers in each *département*, most having incomes of at least 3,000 livres a year. Inclusion on these lists became an insignia of one's informal status as a notable. Members of the electoral colleges and departmental advisory councils were drawn from these lists. Although such honorific positions had little power and no privileges, the designees were effectively co-opted into the regime. Napoleon's Legion of Honour, meanwhile, conferred recognition on men who served the state, primarily military officers who largely stood outside the ranks of the landed notables. By 1814 the Legion had 32,000 members, of whom only 1,500 were civilians.

After Napoleon had himself crowned emperor in 1804, he felt the need for a court aristocracy that would lend lustre and credibility to his new image. He also reasoned that only by creating a new nobility based on merit could he displace and absorb the old nobility, which had lost its titles in 1790 but not its pretensions. By 1808 a new hierarchy of titles had been created, which were to be hereditary provided that a family could support its title with a large annual income—30,000 livres, for example, in the case of a count of the empire. To facilitate this, the emperor bestowed huge landed estates and pensions on his highest dignitaries. The Napoleonic nobility, in other words,

THE FRENCH REVOLUTION, NAPOLEON, AND THE REPUBLIC:
LIBERTÉ, ÉGALITÉ, AND FRATERNITÉ

would be a veritable upper class based on a combination of service and wealth. Predictably, the new nobility was top-heavy with generals (59 percent altogether), but it also included many senators, archbishops, and members of the Conseil d'État; 23 percent of the Napoleonic nobility were former nobles of the ancien régime. These social innovations endured after Napoleon's fall—the Bourbons adopted the system of high-status electoral colleges, maintained the Legion of Honour, and even allowed the Napoleonic nobles to retain their titles alongside the restored old-regime nobility.

THE CIVIL CODE

The Napoleonic Code had a far greater impact on postrevolutionary society than did the social innovations. This ambitious work of legal codification, perhaps the crowning glory of the Conseil d'État, consolidated certain basic principles established in 1789: civil equality and equality before the law; the abolition of feudalism in favour of modern contractual forms of property; and the secularization of civil relations. Codification also made it easier to export those principles beyond the borders of France. In the area of family relations, however, the Napoleonic Code was less a codification of Revolutionary innovations than a reaction against them. By reverting to patriarchal standards that strengthened the prerogatives of the husband and father, it wiped out important gains that women had made during the Revolution. The code's spirit on this subject was summed up in its statement that "a husband owes protection to his wife; a wife owes obedience to her husband." Wives were again barred from signing contracts without their husbands' consent, and a wife's portion of the family's community property fell completely under her husband's control during his lifetime. The code also curbed the right of equal inheritance, which the Revolution had extended even to illegitimate children, and increased the father's disciplinary control over his children.

The code also rolled back the Revolution's extremely liberal divorce legislation. When marriage became a civil rite rather than an obligatory religious sacrament in 1792, divorce became possible for the first time. Divorce could be obtained by mutual consent but also for a range of causes including desertion and simple incompatibility. Under the Napoleonic Code, contested divorce was possible only for unusually cruel treatment resulting in grave injury and for adultery on the part of the wife. Faced with an unfaithful husband, however, "the wife may demand divorce on the ground of adultery by her husband [only] when he shall have brought his concubine into their common residence."

Napoleonic policy frequently reacted against the Revolution's liberal individualism. While the regime did not restore the guilds outright, for example, it reimposed restrictive or even monopolistic state regulation on such occupational groups as publishers and booksellers, the Parisian building trades, attorneys, barristers, notaries, and doctors. Napoleon wished to strengthen the ties that bound individuals together, which derived from religion, the family, and state authority. Napoleon's domestic innovations—the prefectorial system, with its extreme centralization of administrative authority; the university, a centralized educational bureaucracy that scrutinized all types of teachers; the concordat with the Vatican that reversed the secularizing tendencies of the Revolution; the civil code, which strengthened property rights and patriarchal authority; and

THE FRENCH REVOLUTION, NAPOLEON, AND THE REPUBLIC:
LIBERTÉ, ÉGALITÉ, AND FRATERNITÉ

THE NAPOLEONIC CODE BEYOND FRANCE

One of the most evidently lasting effects of the French Revolution was the Napoleonic Code. The French civil code enacted in 1804 and still extant, with revisions, became the main influence in the 19th-century civil codes of most countries of Continental Europe and Latin America.

The code was originally introduced into areas under French control in 1804: Belgium, Luxembourg, parts of western Germany, northwestern Italy, Geneva, and Monaco. It was later introduced into territories conquered by Napoleon: Italy, the Netherlands, the Hanseatic lands, and much of the remainder of western Germany and Switzerland. The code is still in use in Belgium, Luxembourg, and Monaco.

During the 19th century, the Napoleonic Code was voluntarily adopted in a number of European and Latin American countries, either in the form of simple translation or with considerable modifications. The Italian Civil Code of 1865, enacted after the unification of Italy, had a close but indirect relationship with the Napoleonic Code. The new Italian code of 1942 departed to a large extent from this tradition. In Latin America in the early 19th century, the code was introduced into Haiti and the Dominican Republic and is still in force there. Bolivia and Chile followed closely the arrangement of the code and borrowed much of its substance. The Chilean code was in turn copied by Ecuador and Colombia, closely followed by Uruguay and Argentina.

In Louisiana, the only civil-law state in the United States (which is otherwise bound by common law), the civil code of 1825 (revised in 1870 and still in force) is closely connected with the Napoleonic Code. The influence of the Napoleonic Code was diminished at the turn of the century by the introduction of the German Civil Code (1900) and the Swiss Civil Code (1912); the former was adopted by

> Japan and the latter by Turkey. In the 20th century, codes in Brazil, Mexico, Greece, and Peru were products of a comparative method, with ideas borrowed from the German, French, and Swiss.

the Legion of Honour, which rewarded service to the state—all endured in the 19th century despite a succession of political upheavals. Historians who admire Napoleon consider these innovations the "granite masses" on which modern French society developed.

CAMPAIGNS AND CONQUESTS, 1797–1807

Napoleon's sway over France depended from the start on his success in war. After his conquest of northern Italy in 1797 and the dissolution of the first coalition, the Directory intended to invade Britain, France's century-long rival and the last remaining belligerent. Concluding that French naval power could not sustain a seaborne invasion, however, the government sent Napoleon on a military expedition to Egypt instead, hoping to choke off the main route to Britain's Indian empire. When the expedition bogged down in disease and military stalemate, its commander quietly slipped past a British naval blockade to return to France, where (in the absence of accurate news from Egypt) he was received as the nation's leading military hero.

At the time of the Brumaire coup, the republic's armies had been driven from Italy by a second coalition, but they had halted a

THE FRENCH REVOLUTION, NAPOLEON, AND THE REPUBLIC:
LIBERTÉ, ÉGALITÉ, AND FRATERNITÉ

multifront assault on France by the armies of Russia, Austria, and Britain. The republic, in other words, was no longer in imminent military danger, but the prospect of an interminable war loomed on the horizon. After Brumaire the nation expected its new leader to achieve peace through decisive military victory. This promise Napoleon fulfilled, once again leading French armies into northern Italy and defeating Austria at the Battle of Marengo in June 1800. Subsequent defeats in Germany drove Austria to sign the peace treaty of Lunéville in February 1801. Deprived of its Continental allies for the second time, a war-weary Britain finally decided to negotiate. In March 1802 France and Britain signed the Treaty of Amiens, and for the first time in 10 years Europe was at peace.

Within two years, however, the two rivals were again in a state of war. Most historians agree that neither imperial power was solely responsible for the breakdown of this peace, since neither would renounce its ambitions for supremacy. Napoleon repeatedly violated the treaty's spirit—by annexing Piedmont, occupying the Batavian Republic, and assuming the presidency of the Cisalpine Republic. To Britain, the balance of power in Europe required an independent Italy and Dutch Netherlands. Britain violated the letter of the treaty, however, by failing to evacuate the island of Malta as it had promised.

Once again, British naval power frustrated Napoleon's attempt to take the war directly to British soil, and there was little actual fighting until Britain was able to form a new Continental coalition in 1805. At the Battle of Trafalgar (October 21, 1805), British naval gunners decimated the French and Spanish fleets, ending all thought of a cross-Channel invasion. Napoleon turned instead against Britain's Austrian and Russian allies. He surprised the Austrians at Ulm and then smashed them decisively at the Battle of Austerlitz (December 2, 1805), probably his most brilliant tactical feat. Under the Treaty of Pressburg (criticized by the French foreign minister Charles-Maurice de Talleyrand as entirely too harsh), Austria paid a heavy indemnity, ceded its provinces of Venetia and Tyrol, and allowed Napoleon to abolish the Holy Roman Empire. Prussia, kept neutral for a time by vague promises of sovereignty over Hanover, finally mobilized against France, only to suffer humiliating defeats at the Battles of Jena and Auerstädt in October 1806. The French occupied Berlin, levied a huge indemnity on Prussia, seized various provinces, and turned northern Germany into a French sphere of influence. The ensuing campaign against Russia's army in Europe resulted in a bloody stalemate at the Battle of Eylau (February 8, 1807), leaving Napoleon in precarious straits with extremely vulnerable lines of supply. But, when fighting resumed that spring, the French prevailed at the Battle of Friedland (June 14, 1807), and Tsar Alexander I sued for peace. The Treaty of Tilsit, negotiated by the two emperors, divided Europe into two zones of influence, with

Friedland, 1807, oil on canvas by Ernest Meissonier, 1875; Metropolitan Museum of Art, New York.

THE FRENCH REVOLUTION, NAPOLEON, AND THE REPUBLIC:
LIBERTÉ, ÉGALITÉ, AND FRATERNITÉ

Napoleon pledging to aid the Russians against their Ottoman rivals and Alexander promising to cooperate against Britain.

THE GRAND EMPIRE

Napoleon now had a free hand to reorganize Europe and numerous relatives to install on the thrones of his satellite kingdoms. The result was known as the Grand Empire. Having annexed Tuscany, Piedmont, Genoa, and the Rhineland directly into France, Napoleon placed the Kingdom of Holland (which until 1806 was the Batavian Commonwealth) under his brother Louis, the Kingdom of Westphalia under his brother Jérôme, the Kingdom of Italy under his stepson Eugène as his viceroy, the Kingdom of Spain under his brother Joseph, and the Grand Duchy of Warsaw (carved out of Prussian Poland) under the nominal sovereignty of his ally the king of Saxony, Frederick Augustus I. To link his allied states in northern and southern Germany, Napoleon created the Confederation of the Rhine. Even Austria seemed to fall into Napoleon's sphere of influence, with his marriage to Archduchess Marie-Louise in 1810. (Since the emperor had no natural heirs from his marriage to Joséphine Beauharnais, he reluctantly divorced her and in 1810 married the Austrian princess, who duly bore him a son the following year.)

THE CONTINENTAL SYSTEM

Britain, however, was insulated from French military power; only an indirect strategy of economic warfare remained possible. Thus far Britain had driven most French merchant

THE NAPOLEONIC ERA

Europe in 1812.

shipping from the high seas, and in desperation French merchants sold most of their ships to neutrals, allowing the United States to surpass France in the size of its merchant fleet. But after his string of military victories, Napoleon believed that he could choke off British commerce by closing the Continent to its ships and products. With limited opportunities to sell its manufactured goods, he believed,

THE FRENCH REVOLUTION, NAPOLEON, AND THE REPUBLIC:
LIBERTÉ, ÉGALITÉ, AND FRATERNITÉ

the British economy would suffer from overproduction and unemployment, while the lack of foreign gold in payment for British exports would bankrupt the treasury. As France moved into Britain's foreign markets, Britain's economic crisis would drive its government to seek peace. Accordingly, Napoleon launched the "Continental System": in the Berlin Decree of November 1806, he prohibited British trade with all countries under French influence, including British products carried by neutral shipping. When the British retaliated by requiring all neutral ships to stop at British ports for inspection and licenses, Napoleon threatened to seize any ship stopping at English ports. Thus, a total naval war against neutrals erupted.

Economic warfare took its toll on all sides. While France did make inroads in cotton manufacturing in the absence of British competition, France and especially its allies suffered terribly from the British blockade, in particular from a dearth of colonial raw materials. The great Atlantic ports of Nantes, Bordeaux, and Amsterdam never recovered, as ancillary industries such as shipbuilding and sugar refining collapsed. The axis of European trade shifted decisively inland. The Continental System did strain the British economy, driving down exports and gold reserves in 1810, but the blockade was extremely porous. Because Europeans liked British goods, smugglers had incentive to evade the restrictions in such places as Spain and Portugal. By 1811, moreover, a restive Tsar Alexander withdrew from the Continental System. Thus, the most dire effect of the Continental System was the stimulus it gave Napoleon for a new round of aggression against Portugal, Spain, and Russia.

By 1810 almost 300,000 imperial troops were bogged down in Iberia, struggling against a surprisingly vigorous Spanish resistance and a British expeditionary force. Then, in 1812, Napoleon embarked on his most quixotic aggression—an invasion of Russia designed to humble "the colossus of Northern barbarism" and exclude Russia from any influence in Europe. The Grand Army of 600,000 men that crossed into Russia reached Moscow without inflicting a decisive defeat on the Russian armies. By the time Napoleon on October 19 belatedly ordered a retreat from Moscow, which had been burned to the ground and was unfit for winter quarters, he had lost two-thirds of his troops from disease, battle casualties, cold, and hunger. The punishing retreat through the Russian winter killed most of the others. Yet this unparalleled disaster did not humble or discourage the emperor. Napoleon believed that he could hold his empire together and defeat yet another anti-French coalition that was forming. He correctly assumed that he could still rely on his well-honed administrative bureaucracy to replace the decimated Grand Army.

CONSCRIPTION

Building on the Directory's conscription law of September 1798, the Napoleonic regime, after considerable trial and error, had created the mechanisms for imposing on the citizens of France and the annexed territories the distasteful obligation of military service. Each year the Ministry of War Administration assigned a quota of conscripts for every *département*. Using communal birth registers, the mayor of each commune compiled a list of men reaching the age of 19 that year. After a preliminary examination to screen out the manifestly unfit and those below the minimum height of 5 feet 1 inch (1.5 metres), the young men

THE FRENCH REVOLUTION, NAPOLEON, AND THE REPUBLIC:
LIBERTÉ, ÉGALITÉ, AND FRATERNITÉ

drew numbers in a lottery at the cantonal seat. Doctors in the departmental capitals later ruled on other claims for medical exemptions, and in all about a third of the youths avoided military service legally as physically unfit. Though married men were not exempt from the draft, two other means of avoiding induction remained, apart from drawing a high number: the wealthy could purchase a replacement, and the poor could flee.

For Napoleon's prefects, the annual conscription levy was the top priority and draft evasion the number-one problem in most *départements*. Persistence, routine stepped-up policing, and coercion gradually overcame the chronic resistance. Napoleon had begun by drafting 60,000 Frenchmen annually, but by 1810 the quota hit 120,000, and the first of many "supplementary levies" was decreed to call up men from earlier classes who had drawn high numbers. In January 1813, after the Russian disaster, Napoleon replenished his armies by calling up the class of 1814 a year early and by repeated supplementary levies. Because he could still rely on his conscription machine, Napoleon consistently rebuffed offers by the allies to negotiate peace. Only after he lost the decisive Battle of Leipzig in October 1813 and was driven back across the Rhine did the machine break down. His call of November 1813 for 300,000 more men went largely unfilled. With the troops at his disposal, the emperor fought the Battle of France skillfully, but he could not stop the allies. Shortly after Paris fell, he abdicated, on April 6, 1814, and departed for the island of Elba. France was reduced to its 1792 borders, and the Bourbons returned to the throne. Altogether—along with large levies of Italians, Germans, and other foreigners from the annexed territories and satellite states—nearly 2,500,000 Frenchmen had been drafted by Napoleon, and at least 1,000,000 of these conscripts never returned, roughly half that number being casualties and the other half imprisoned or missing.

The most sympathetic explanation for Napoleon's relentless aggression holds that he was responding to the irreducible antagonism of Britain: French power and glory were the only antidotes to John Bull's arrogance. Others have argued that Napoleon's vendetta against Britain was merely a rationalization for a mad 10-year chase across Europe to establish a new version of Charlemagne's empire. This "imperial design" thesis, however, makes sense only in 1810, as a way Napoleon might have organized his conquests and not as the motivation for them. (Only retrospectively did Napoleon write, "There will be no repose for Europe until she is under only one Head…an Emperor who should distribute kingdoms among his lieutenants.") In the end, one is thrown back on the explanation of temperament. In his combination of pragmatism and insatiable ambition, this world-historic figure remains an enigma. Increasingly "aristocratic" at home and "imperial" abroad, Napoleon was obviously something more than the "general of the Revolution." And yet, with civil code in one hand and sabre in the other, Napoleon could still be seen by Europeans as a personification on both counts of the French Revolution's explosive force.

NAPOLEON AND THE REVOLUTION

The Revolutionary legacy for Napoleon consisted above all in the abolition of the ancien régime's most archaic features—"feudalism," seigneurialism, legal privileges, and provincial

THE FRENCH REVOLUTION, NAPOLEON, AND THE REPUBLIC:
LIBERTÉ, EGALITÉ, AND FRATERNITÉ

liberties. No matter how aristocratic his style became, he had no use for the ineffective institutions and abuses of the ancien régime. Napoleon was "modern" in temperament as well as destructively aggressive. But in either guise he was an authoritarian, with little patience for argument, who profited from the Revolution's clearing operations to construct and mobilize in his own fashion. His concept of reform exaggerated the Revolution's emphasis on uniformity and centralization. Napoleon also accepted the Revolutionary principles of civil equality and equality of opportunity, meaning the recognition of merit. Other rights and liberties did not seem essential. Unlike others before him who had tried and failed, Napoleon terminated the Revolution, but at the price of suppressing the electoral process and partisan politics altogether. Toward the end of the empire, his centralizing vision took over completely, reinforcing his personal will to power. France was merely a launching pad for Napoleon's boundless military and imperial ambition, its prime function being to raise men and money for war. In utter contrast to the Revolution, then, militarism became the defining quality of the Napoleonic regime.

Napoleon's ambiguous legacy helps explain the dizzying events that shook France in 1814 and 1815. Even before Napoleon's abdication, the Imperial Senate, led by the former foreign minister Talleyrand, had begun negotiations with the allies to ensure a transition to a regime that would protect the positions of those who had gained from the Revolution and the Napoleonic period. Louis XVI's long-exiled brother was allowed to return as King Louis XVIII, but he had to agree to rule under a constitution (called the Charter) that provided for legislative control over budgets and taxes and guaranteed

THE NAPOLEONIC ERA

Napoleon's eventual defeat and abdication led to his exile, first to Elba in 1814, and subsequently to St. Helena in 1815 (illustrated in this undated print), where he died in 1821.

THE FRENCH REVOLUTION, NAPOLEON, AND THE REPUBLIC:
LIBERTÉ, EGALITÉ, AND FRATERNITÉ

basic liberties. However, the Bourbons alienated the officer corps by retiring many at half pay and frightened many citizens by not making clear how much of their property and power the church and émigrés would regain. As the anti-Napoleonic allies argued among themselves about the spoils of war, Napoleon slipped back to France for a last adventure, believing that he could reach Paris without firing a shot. At various points along the way, troops disobeyed royalist officers and rallied to the emperor, while Louis fled the country. Between March and June 1815—a period known as the Hundred Days—Napoleon again ruled France. Contrary to his expectation, however, the allies patched up their differences and were determined to rout "the usurper." At the Battle of Waterloo (June 18, 1815) British and Prussian forces defeated Napoleon's army decisively, and he abdicated again a few days later. Placed on the remote island of St. Helena in the South Atlantic, he died in 1821. The "Napoleonic legend"—the retrospective version of events created by Napoleon during his exile—burnished his image in France for decades to come. But in the final analysis Napoleon's impact on future generations was not nearly as powerful as the legacy of the French Revolution itself.

CONCLUSION

The French Revolution marks an essential turning point in the history of global revolutions as well as in the rise of modernity. While the Revolution's ultimate culmination in the reign of Napoleon—who became a despot in his own right—followed by a restoration of the monarchy may make it appear as though the patriots had failed to fully realize their goal of overthrowing an absolutist form of government, the true legacy of the French Revolution was the way in which it fundamentally restructured the social order.

While Napoleon's reign may have reached tyranny at its worst, as a figure himself Napoleon never became king. His actions and position were never considered to be sanctified or ordained by God. Government, politics, and the structure of society were no longer thought to be controlled by divine ordinance or an invisible hand; the demystification had begun, and the men and women of France had shown the world the inherent power that lay within each individual, regardless of class or status. Even the restoration of the monarchy under King Louis XVIII in 1814 was seen not as divine will but rather a practical measure to end war and ensure normalcy for the people.

In years since, the French Revolution has served as an inspiration to countless subsequent insurrections. The War of Greek Independence (1821–32) the Latin American wars of independence (1808–1826), and the Russian Revolution of 1917 all drew on the rhetoric and ideals of the French Revolution. The close intellectual exchange between Thomas Jefferson and the Marquis de Lafayette before and during the American

THE FRENCH REVOLUTION, NAPOLEON, AND THE REPUBLIC:
LIBERTÉ, ÉGALITÉ, AND FRATERNITÉ

and French Revolutions speaks to the way in which the two figures mutually influenced each other. A comparison of the French Declaration of the Rights of Man and of the Citizen with the United States' own Bill of Rights, enacted within two years of each other, shows that.

At home the French Revolution ultimately unified the country, but its global implications were far wider reaching. It gave birth to a dominant middle class and marked the beginnings of militant nationalism. It ushered in the end of feudalism and the birth of a new social order through the Napoleonic Code and the Declaration of the Rights of Man and of the Citizen. The revolutionary motto "*Liberté, égalité, fraternité*" ("Freedom, equality, brotherhood") remains just as powerful today as it was in 1789.

GLOSSARY

ANCIEN RÉGIME The political and social system of France before the Revolution of 1789.

ARBITRATION The settling of a dispute in which both sides present their arguments to a third person or group for settlement.

ARRONDISSEMENT The largest division of a French department.

ASSIGNAT A bill issued as currency by the French Revolutionary government (1789–96) on the security of expropriated lands.

BIENS NATIONAUX Formerly church- or émigré-owned property in France that, by vote of the National Assembly, was designated as national lands then sold to pay off national debt.

CAHIER A report or memorial embodying resolutions or instructions concerning policy especially of a parliamentary body.

CAPITATION A direct uniform tax imposed upon each head or person.

CAPITULATE To stop trying to fight or resist something.

CIVIL LAW Laws that deal with the rights of people rather than with crimes.

CONSUL One of the chief magistrates of the French republic from 1799 to 1804 or of one of the Italian republics established upon the French pattern.

DÉCADE One of the three periods of 10 days into which each 30-day month was divided on the French republican calendar.

DEMAGOGUE A political leader who tries to get support by making false claims and promises and using arguments based on emotion rather than reason.

DÉPARTEMENT The largest administrative subdivision in France and some of the French colonies presided over by a prefect.

THE FRENCH REVOLUTION, NAPOLEON, AND THE REPUBLIC:
LIBERTÉ, EGALITÉ, AND FRATERNITÉ

ÉMIGRÉ A person who is forced to leave a country for political reasons.

ENLIGHTENMENT A movement of the 18th century that stressed the belief that science and logic give people more knowledge and understanding than tradition and religion.

ESTATE One of two or more great classes or orders of a state regarded as part of the body politic who are vested with distinct political powers and whose concurrence is necessary for legislation.

ESTATES-GENERAL A legislative assembly composed of members or representatives of the estates of a nation as distinguished from the states provincial (such as the legislative assembly of France before the Revolution or the legislative assembly of the Netherlands from the 15th century to 1796).

EXPEDITIOUS Acting or done in a quick and efficient way.

FEUDALISM A social system that existed in Europe during the Middle Ages in which people worked and fought for nobles who gave them protection and the use of land in return.

JURISPRUDENCE A system or body of law.

LAISSEZ-FAIRE A doctrine opposing governmental interference in economic affairs beyond the minimum necessary for the maintenance of peace and property rights.

LETTRE DE CACHET A letter signed by the king of France and countersigned by a secretary of state and used primarily to authorize someone's imprisonment.

PARLEMENT One of several principal courts of justice existing in France before the Revolution of 1789.

PHYSIOCRAT A member of a school of political economists founded in 18th century France and characterized chiefly by a belief that government policy should not interfere with the operation of natural economic laws and that land is the source of all wealth.

PREFECT A chief officer or government official who is responsible for a particular area in some countries.

RAPPROCHEMENT The development of friendlier relations between countries or groups of people who have been enemies.

SANSCULOTTE An extreme radical republican in France at the time of the French Revolution.

SEIGNEURIALISM Also known as manorialism, a system of economic, social, and political organization based on the medieval manor, or seigneurie.

TAILLE A royal or a national tax in 15th-century France from which the lords and later the clergy and others were exempt.

THIRD ESTATE The third of the traditional political orders; specifically: the commons.

BIBLIOGRAPHY

A great historian's review of the long sweep of French history, from prehistoric times to the modern era, is Fernand Braudel, *The Identity of France*, 2nd ed. (1988–90, originally published in French, 1986), and *The Identity of France: People and Production* (1990; originally published in French, 1986). Excellent thematic treatments are provided in Marc Bloch, *French Rural Society: An Essay on Its Basic Characteristics* (1966; originally published in French, 1931), a classic study; Fernand Braudel and Ernest Labrousse (eds.), *Histoire économique et sociale de la France* (1970–82); Georges Duby and Armand Wallon (eds.), *Histoire de la France rurale*, 4 vol. (1975–76, reprinted 1992); and Georges Duby (ed.), *Histoire de la France urbaine*, 5 vol. (1980–85).

ON PREREVOLUTIONARY FRANCE (1715-1789)

Alexis de Tocqueville, *The Old Régime and the French Revolution* (1955, reprinted 1978; originally published in French, 1856), is still a basic source for the study of the period. Comprehensive histories include Daniel Roche, *France in the Enlightenment* (1998; originally published in French, 1993), a detailed survey of the period's society and culture; and vol. 1 of Alfred Cobban, *A History of Modern France*, 3 vol. (1969). Michel Antoine, *Louis XV* (1989), is both a biography and an exhaustive account of high politics in that monarch's reign. Guy Chaussinand-Nogaret, *The French Nobility in the Eighteenth Century* (1985; originally published in French, 1986), explains the changing nature of the country's ruling elite.

Steven Laurence Kaplan, *Provisioning Paris: Merchants and Millers in the Grain and Flour Trade During the Eighteenth Century* (1984), describes a basic feature of the period's economy. Economic histories make much use of the 18th-century travelogue of Arthur Young, *Travels During the Years 1787, 1788, & 1789: Undertaken More Particularly with a View of Ascertaining the Cultivation, Wealth, Resources, and National Prosperity of the Kingdom of France*, 2nd ed., 2 vol. (1794), available in many later editions. There are fascinating glimpses of urban life in Louis-Sébastien Mercier, *Panorama of Paris: Selections from Tableau de Paris* (1999; originally published in French, 1781); and Jacques-Louis Ménétra, *Journal of My Life* (1986; originally published in French, 1982). The culture and ideology of the period are explored in Robert Darnton, *The Forbidden Best-Sellers of Pre-Revolutionary France* (1995); Lieselotte Steinbrügge, *The Moral Sex: Woman's Nature in the French Enlightenment* (1995; originally published in German, 1992); Dena Goodman, *The Republic of Letters: A Cultural History of the French Enlightenment* (1994); and Thomas E. Crow, *Painters and Public Life in Eighteenth-Century Paris* (1985). David Bell, *The Cult of the Nation* (2001), offers an important new analysis of the growth of national identity. A classic analysis of his thought is Jean Starobinski, *Jean-Jacques Rousseau; Transparency and Obstruction* (1988; originally published in French, 1957). Keith Michael Baker, *Inventing the French Revolution* (1990); and Dale K. Van Kley, *The Religious Origins of the French Revolution* (1996), show how revolutionary ideas developed out of prerevolutionary political discourse.

ON THE REVOLUTION AND NAPOLEON (1789–1815)

Reliable overviews of the period include D. M. G. Sutherland, *France 1789–1815: Revolution and Counter-Revolution* (1985); William Doyle, *The Oxford History of the French Revolution* (1989);

and Norman Hampson, *A Social History of the French Revolution* (1963, reissued 1995).

On the origins of the Revolution, see Jean Egret, *The French Pre-Revolution* (1977; originally published in French, 1962); and William Doyle, *Origins of the French Revolution*, 3rd ed. (1998). The best book on the Terror is still R. R. Palmer, *Twelve Who Ruled: The Year of the Terror in the French Revolution* (1941, reissued 1989). George Rudé, *Robespierre* (1967), provides excerpts from the Jacobin leader's speeches. Martyn Lyons, *France Under the Directory* (1975), surveys the Revolution's later phase. François Furet and Mona Ozouf (eds.), *A Critical Dictionary of the French Revolution* (1989; originally published in French, 1988), is an important and original collection of short essays on selected events, actors, institutions, ideas, and historians of the French Revolution. Lynn Hunt, *Politics, Culture, and Class in the French Revolution* (1984), analyzes the imagery and sociology of revolutionary politics. Notable thematic studies include Georges Lefebvre, *The Great Fear of 1789: Rural Panic in Revolutionary France* (1973, reissued 1989; originally published in French, 1932); P. M. Jones, *The Peasantry in the French Revolution* (1988); Albert Soboul, *The Parisian Sans-culottes and the French Revolution*, 1793–4, trans. from French (1964, reprinted 1979); George Rudé, *The Crowd in the French Revolution* (1959, reprinted 1986); Dominique Godineau, *The Women of Paris and Their French Revolution* (1998; originally published in French, 1988); John McManners, *The French Revolution and the Church* (1969, reprinted 1982); Jean-Paul Bertaud, *The Army of the French Revolution* (1988; originally published in French, 1979); Emmet Kennedy, *A Cultural History of the French Revolution* (1989); and Jacques Godechot, *The Counter-Revolution: Doctrine and Action*,

1789–1804 (1971, reissued 1981; originally published in French, 1961). The international dimension of the Revolution is interpreted in R. R. Palmer, *The World of the French Revolution* (1971). The best biography of a revolutionary leader is Leo Gershoy, *Bertrand Barère: A Reluctant Terrorist* (1962). John Hardman, *Louis XVI* (1993), is a life of the movement's most illustrious victim; and the reasons for his fate are explained in David Jordan, *The King's Trial* (1979, reprinted 1993). Isser Woloch, *The New Regime* (1994), shows how the Revolution's principles were institutionalized. Jeremy D. Popkin, *Revolutionary News* (1990), explains the "media revolution" that was an integral part of the upheaval after 1789.

Martyn Lyons, *Napoleon Bonaparte and the Legacy of the French Revolution* (1994), is a good overview. On Napoleon's life, see Felix Markham, *Napoleon* (1963); Jean Tulard, *Napoleon: The Myth of the Saviour* (1984; originally published in French, 1977); and Geoffrey Ellis, *Napoleon* (1997, reissued 2000). The best volume on the Napoleonic regime in France is Louis Bergeron, *France Under Napoleon* (1981; originally published in French, 1972). Owen Connelly, *Blundering to Glory: Napoleon's Military Campaigns*, rev. ed. (1999), is a critical and incisive analysis. For the views of historians across the generations, see Pieter Geyl, *Napoleon: For and Against* (1949, reissued 1976; originally published in Dutch, 1946).

INDEX

A

Affair of the Diamond Necklace, 39–41
agriculture, 11, 17, 30
    patterns in, 11–12
American Revolution, 1, 27, 135–136
ancien régime
    colonialism under, 14–15, 25
    death of, 60
    definition of, 2
    efforts at reform of, 24–25
    factors leading to dissolution of, 41, 43
    failures of, 49
    flags of, 56
    institutions of, 34, 45, 65, 65, 132
    law of, 9
    nobles of, 120
    origin of term, 1
    peculiarity of, 6
    social order of, 2–4, 131
    society of, 19
    use of lettres de cachet under, 9
Army of the Republic, 96–98, 129
arrondissements, 113–114
Assembly of Notables, 39, 41, 42
assignats, 68
    inflation of, 68, 83, 99, 105–106

B

Babeuf, François Noël, 100, 101–102
Barère, Bertrand, 85, 86, 98
Bastille, 8, 9, 41
    fall of, 1, 57
    storming of, 49, 54–55
Belgium, annexation of, 80, 103, 122
biens nationaux, 68, 118
Brissot, Jacques-Pierre, 29, 73, 76–77, 83, 84
Brissotins, 83, 84
Brunswick Manifesto, 77

C

cahiers de doléances, 42–43, 52
Calas, Jean, 18
calendar, republican, 92–93, 116
Calonne, Charles-Alexandre de, 38–39, 41–42
capitation, 31, 34–35

citizenship, 2, 3
    relationship to state, 24
    Rousseau's ideas about, 21
Civil Constitution of the Clergy, 71, 72
civil law, 65, 116, 122
clergy, 2, 42–43, 44, 50–51, 52, 53, 59, 71, 74, 77, 80, 82, 102, 116, 118
    "constitutional priests," 71, 72, 94
    exemption from taxes of, 34
    "refractory priests," 71, 72, 74, 76–77, 80, 82, 102, 116
clubs, 74
    Club Breton, 73
    Club of the Cordeliers, 73, 76
    Club of the Feuillants, 76, 77, 78
    Jacobin, 63, 73, 74, 76, 83, 84, 85, 93–94
    Neo-Jacobins, 102–103
    political, 72, 74, 114
    provincial, 76
    reading, 74
    revolutionary, 73
    women's, 63

Colbert, Jean-Baptiste, 6, 25
commerce, 10, 14–16, 30, 44
    British, 127
Committee of Public Safety, 85, 89, 91, 93, 98
conscription, 106–107, 114, 129–131
Conseil d'État, 112–113, 120
Constituent Assembly, 9
constitution, 8, 10, 38–39, 52, 60, 61, 63, 78, 79, 89, 102, 107–108, 112, 115, 132, 134
    compromise with, 76
    defenders of, 107
    English, 18–19
    of Jacobins, 89–90
    liberties of, 87
Constitution of 1791, 76, 78, 110
Constitution of 1793, 99, 101–102
Constitution of Year III (1795), 99–100, 101, 103
Constitution of the Year VIII, 110
Constitution of the Year XII (May 1804), 110
constitutionalism, 1
constitutional monarchy, 48, 52

NAPOLEON, AND THE REPUBLIC:
LIBERTÉ, EGALITÉ, AND FRATERNITÉ

Consulate, 109, 110, 112–114, 115, 116

Continental System, 126–129

Corps Legislatif, 110, 112

D

Danton, Georges, 84, 94

Declaration of the Rights of Man and of the Citizen, 60, 136

départements, 63–64, 65, 69, 70, 71, 82, 84, 85, 87, 89, 96, 100, 102, 103, 113–114, 115, 119, 129, 130

Diderot, Denis, 18, 22

Directory, 93, 99–100, 102–103, 104, 106, 107, 110, 114, 123

    conscription law of, 129

    foreign policy of, 106

E

education, 20–21, 33, 74, 89, 98, 116, 121, 123

electoral assemblies, 103, 113

    Paris, 84

emigration, 70

Encyclopédistes, 18, 47

Enlightenment, 16, 17, 18, 19, 23, 25, 28, 36, 38, 44, 46–47

Estates-General, 9, 33, 42, 43, 45, 49, 50, 51, 52, 57, 58, 61

F

famine, 10, 99

feudalism, 103, 120, 131–132, 136

    abolition of, 59–60

Frederick Augustus I, 126

Frederick II (the Great), 25, 26–27

G

Girondins, 29, 38, 44, 83–88, 94, 98

Grand Empire, 126

guilds, 3, 28, 45, 65, 121

    abolition of, 37

H

Hébert, Jacques-René, 88, 94

Hundred Days, 134

I

individualism, 1, 28, 38, 65, 121

industry, 12–13, 16, 128

    bourgeois control of, 44

J

Jacobins, 63, 73, 74, 76–77, 81–82, 83, 84, 85, 87, 88, 90, 91, 97, 98, 99, 101–102, 114–115
- constitution of, 89–90
- democracy of, 21
- dictatorship of, 92–96

Jesuits, 20, 36

Jews, 5, 118

jurisprudence, 65

L

Lafayette, marquis de, 27, 73, 77, 135–136
- command of national guard, 76

laissez-faire doctrine, 17, 37, 65

Legion of Honour, 119, 120, 121, 123

Legislative Assembly
- beginning of, 76
- conflict with militants, 77–78
- election of, 61–62
- loss of mandate of, 78
- military actions of, 77
- passing laws in, 62
- suspension of the king, 78

lettres de cachet, 8–9, 38

lettres de grâce, 9

Louis XIII, 6, 28

Louis XIV, 6–7, 28
- death of, 18, 25, 35
- foreign policy of, 25
- *grand siècle* of, 10, 21

Louis XV, 17, 26, 36, 40
- comptroller general of, 32
- death of, 36
- sexual adventures of, 39

Louis XVI, 17, 36–37, 39, 40, 41, 42, 53, 57, 74, 75–76, 77
- attempt to flee, 74–75
- brother of, 132, 134
- execution of, 81–82
- failure of, 48, 49, 52
- finance minister of, 30
- inability to consummate marriage, 39

Louis XVIII, 135

lynching, 55, 57, 80, 90, 98–99

M

Maupeou, René-Nicolas-Charles-Augustin de, 33, 36–37
   dismissal of, 37, 38
Marat, Jean-Paul, 74, 80, 84
Marie-Antoinette, 39, 40, 41, 77
Maximum, 89
modernization, 6–8, 10, 30, 56
monarchy
   appeal to public, 23
   and the church, 5–6
   critics of, 21, 77
   development of absolute monarchy, 6, 7
   economic policies of, 7–8, 34, 35
   efforts at reform of, 30, 32, 39, 52, 61, 62
   factors in collapse of, 27, 42, 46, 47
   failure to adapt of, 2, 24–25, 28, 47, 48, 52
   foreign policy of, 25
   image problem of, 39, 40
   judicial system of, 53
   overthrow of, 79, 80, 90
   restoration of, 132, 135
Montagnards, 44, 83–88, 90, 98, 99
Montesquieu, baron de La Brède et de, 18–23, 28, 35

N

Napoleon Bonaparte, 65, 104, 107, 108, 135
   abdication of, 130, 132
   anti-Napoleonic forces, 134
   campaigns and conquests of, 123–126
   coup d'état of, 93
   defeat at Waterloo, 134
   era of, 93, 109–110, 112–116, 118–121, 123–132, 134
   legend of, 134
   nobility during rule of, 119–120
   relationship to Revolution, 131–132, 134
   return to rule of, 134
   society during rule of, 115–116
Napoleonic Code, 120–121, 122–123, 136
National Assembly
   beginning of, 49, 52, 73

constitution under, 61

conflict within, 62

criticism of, 70

dissolution of, 76

economic system of, 59, 60, 65, 68

judicial system of, 65

military of, 96

new regime under, 60–61

politics under, 62, 63, 72, 73, 74, 75–76, 110

presidents of, 29, 53

religious tensions under, 59, 62, 71

rescue of by peasants, 53, 57, 58, 59

taxation under, 70

tension with king, 53

views on women, 63

National Convention

assembly of, 79, 80

conflicts, 82, 83, 84, 85–87, 88–89, 90, 98, 99

constitution of, 89, 90

declarations of, 82, 92, 94, 96, 97–98, 100, 110

economic problems of, 83

elections of, 78, 83, 84

trial of Louis XVI, 80–82

Necker, Jacques, 4, 29, 43, 49, 54

Neo-Jacobins, 102–103, 107

newspapers, 15, 23, 72–73, 74, 97, 103, 115

nobility, 2, 5, 30, 34, 36, 42–43, 44–45, 50–51, 52, 53, 58–59, 62–63, 70, 74, 82–83

distinction with bourgeoisie, 44

exemption from taxes of, 31, 34, 41

land ownership of, 11–12, 58

Napoleonic, 119–120

"nobility of the robe," 35

P

Paris Commune, 77–78, 80, 84, 85, 88, 94, 96

Parlement of Bordeaux, 18

Parlement of Britanny, 36

Parlement of Paris, 6, 38, 41, 43

parlements, 8, 10, 31, 32–33, 35–36, 61

judges of, 52

the king and, 36–39, 41–43

peasants, 3–4, 15, 37, 38, 45, 54, 59, 60, 65, 68–69, 70, 74, 82–83, 89, 90
   debtors, 118
   economic status of, 11
   growth of population, 11
   insurgencies of, 57–59
   land ownership of, 11–12, 45, 60, 68, 69
   taxes paid by, 34
Pétion, Jérôme, 76, 84
physiocrats, 17, 37
pope, 5, 18, 118
   Pius VII, 116
prefect, 113–114, 121, 123, 130
   clergy as moral prefects, 118
Protestants, 5, 12, 17–18, 29, 37–38
   pastors, 118

R

rationality, 1
Reign of Terror, 88–91, 93, 101
Revolutionary Tribunal, 85, 86–87, 89, 94
Richelieu, cardinal and duke de, 6
   death of, 6–7
Robespierre, Maximilien, 73, 76, 80, 83, 84, 90–91, 93, 94, 95–96
   fall of, 98, 101
Roland, Jean-Marie, 84
Roman Catholic Church
   exemption from taxes of, 31
   land ownership of, 11–12, 58, 68, 71, 118, 134
   relationship with monarchy, 5–6
   reconciliation with, 116, 118
   Rousseau's criticism of, 20
   tensions with Revolution, 71–72, 94, 106
   tithe of, 59
Rousseau, Jean-Jacques, 16–17, 18, 19, 21
   concern for education of, 20
   Émile, 6, 20
   ideas of, 22
royalists, constitutional, 73

S

Saint-Just, Louis de, 91, 96
salons, 20, 23, 84
   politics of, 115
sansculottes, 84, 85, 87, 89, 90, 93, 97, 98–99, 114–115
School of Bridges and Roads, 29
sectional assemblies, 88

seigneurialism, 131–132
Seven Years' War, 14, 26
Sieyès, Emmanuel-Joseph, 43, 51, 62, 107, 108, 109, 112
Society of the Friends of the Constitution, 73
subprefects, 114

T

taille, 31, 34–35
Talleyrand, Charles-Maurice de, 125, 132
tariffs, 3, 15, 65
taxes
    aides, 31
    capitation, 34–35
    collection of, 37, 42, 114, 119
    exemptions from, 29, 41
    gabelle, 31
    necessary for franchise, 63, 99–100
    paulette, 35
    reform of, 31–33, 49, 70, 97, 132, 135
    royal, 58
    taille, 34–35
    traites, 31
    vingtième, 31
    from war, 103
Terray, Joseph-Marie, 32, 33
    reforms of, 36
Thermidorian Convention, 99
Thermidorian Reactin, 98–100, 106
Third Estate, 2, 50, 52, 53, 57, 59
    pamphlet about, 43, 51
    radical deputies of, 51, 52, 73
traditionalism, 1, 25, 28
Tribunate, 110, 112, 115
Turgot, Anne-Robert-Jacques, 21, 28–29, 37, 38, 47
    reforms of, 45
Two-Thirds Decree, 100, 102

V

Vendée rebellion, 82, 95

W

War of the Austrian Succession, 25, 31

NAPOLEON, AND THE REPUBLIC:
LIBERTÉ, EGALITÉ, AND FRATERNITÉ